Safety Program Management

"Proof of Concept"

David James Nolting, MS

ISBN 979-8-88685-158-8 (paperback)
ISBN 979-8-88685-992-8 (hardcover)
ISBN 979-8-88685-159-5 (digital)

Christian Faith Publishing
832 Park Avenue
Meadville, PA 16335
www.christianfaithpublishing.com

Printed in the United States of America

Contents

Preface

After many years of experience and observation in the safety profession, I felt compelled to write a book that would assist and benefit safety managers across the industry spectrum in a realistic way for those that do not have the resources or network to learn from and support their efforts. In this book, I do not discuss in any great detail all the governmental regulations but rather a full complement of ideas and strategies that I have come to embrace and utilize throughout my thirty-three years of managing safety programs for some of the most challenging and risky environments. I feel a need to share many of my successes, as well as shortcomings, so that the reader can have a resource of proven concepts that may elevate their performance while providing a sound posture for safe work practices, conditions, with an added measure of emotional intelligence.

Over the years, there have only been a couple of safety professionals that I can truly say I considered to be either a mentor or a credible leader in the safety field. I have known many very good people who were charged with the responsibility of providing guidance and administrative support for the safety of a business but, in my opinion, fell short in both areas due to a lack of understanding of people and systems. This book is intended to support those who would like to delve into the minds of their workforce and understand the processes and mechanisms of creating a system that address their specific needs.

My unique beginnings in the safety business, with a background in law enforcement as an accident investigator, allowed me to excel throughout my safety career in a manner that seemed to flow through a path of understanding that encouraged me to learn as much as I could with a passion to always try new ways of achieving safety excellence. Being a member of law enforcement elevated my communication skills, giving me the ability to listen and not jump to conclusions based on assumptions about what I was being told or what I thought I knew. This also trained me to talk intelligently and relate with many levels of the community, in both speech and written word. My problem-solving skills were raised due to training and experience in dealing with crisis situations, many times being the first on the scene making split-second decisions. I learned quickly that the human aspect to achieving an acceptable level of safety was at the root to my success. I never stopped learning!

Last, but not the least, at the end of this book is an appendix titled "Counseling Influences in Occupational Safety," which is a research paper I wrote while acquiring my master's in counseling in 1998. I added this paper to show where some of my motivation and ideas came from regarding the human aspect to safety management.

Chapter 1

The New Safety Manager

There's a variety of ways and reasons for how and why a person becomes the safety manager of a business. Some circumstances may lead to a senior employee, or valued worker, being selected to take on that business's safety responsibilities. Sometimes, someone already employed may be given added responsibilities in parallel to their already heavy workload. Some come right out of college with a degree in safety, with an added distinction of being a Certified Safety Professional (CSP) as part of the learning and testing curriculum. Whatever the circumstances are, there's one thing in common that we all have, and that is the responsibility for the health, safety, and well-being of the workforce we serve.

It's not just a job, it's a position that requires wearing many different hats. One day you're a teacher, the next a counselor, then on to the administrator roll, technical writer, as well as an investigator. You are the one that has to answer the tough questions and must have the right answers…always. You are the person who interfaces with the customers, regulatory agencies, authorities, suppliers, workforce, insurance agents/adjusters, medical staff, subcontractors, and last but not least, the public when working in their communities.

The safety manager is responsible to ensure that you are addressing the hazards that your workforce is exposed to and that the system that is in place mitigates those risks to an acceptable and required level. So for the new safety manager, this needs to be the bases for your system. The new safety manager should develop a game plan to create a specific system that focuses on your unique risks and needs.

There are many options and opinions that guide one through the task of identifying the risks associated with the workforce that you represent. Some come from regulatory compliance (fed and state) while others are adopted through alike industry standards and best practices. Whatever is your guiding source, remember that what you put in writing is what you are held to. To this point, I would recommend that when creating your safety program, only incorporate what you can realistically enforce and control and what is truly needed or required. Adopting safety plans from another company and stating that they are your company's rules for safety can lead to many headaches if not carefully vetted. I've seen adopted programs being written and sent out to customers for auditing purposes without really knowing what exactly the plan requires of their workforce. Remember…if you have it in writing, then OSHA, MSHA, etc. will hold you to that rule even if it is not one of their mandates. As we all know, the flip side is that your program must be at least as stringent as the regulatory agencies…should be more but never less!

If safety is a profession that you wish to pursue, then step back and take a look at all the many different paths that this career field has to offer. There's more to being a safety professional than being a manager. You might be more comfortable specializing in only one or a couple of areas of expertise. The many paths include training, industrial hygiene, inspections, technician, marine chemist, engineering, enforcement, consultant, insurance loss prevention, construction, general industry, marine, shipyard, agriculture, manufacturing, program management, medical, or director of a multifaceted safety environment. Although this list is not all inclusive of the many more sources of safety-related career paths, these are the most common that are available without joining the military. What path you take is up to you, but taken with commitment and passion can lead to a rewarding experience that most other careers cannot match.

I believe that the most important recommendation that I can give is to create value to your position. Sure, company management realizes, in most cases, that having a safety professional on board is a requirement to help satisfy customers and regulatory agencies, as well as providing a safe workplace for its employees. In an effort to secure your employment, you need to elevate your worth or value to the company. Elevating your value comes from doing the behind the scene work of protecting the company from itself. What do I mean by this? Simply put, company management can sometimes be their own worst enemy when it comes to managing or recognizing risk. It is because of this understanding we should all have, that we need to ensure that management is aware of the assumptions that they may have of their workforce's safety and to always try and steer their attention toward supporting your efforts. By displaying a professional attitude and managing the safety risk to the company will help them realize that the true investment in you is not only for the proactive work you do but also for the professional attention that you will be able to offer in a time of crises. It was once said that the true cost of professionalism is realized when hiring an amature to manage a crisis.

Remember, the safety manager does not live on an island...you need to solicit the help of others so that safety can be managed with a team approach to what I call safety assurance (S/A).

As you read through this book, I would hope that you gain some knowledge that helps in some of your decision-making when establishing that specific safety program...the one that fits your interest and passion. If you follow any advice I give in this book, please pay close attention to the chapters on emotional intelligence and leadership.

Chapter 2

The Experienced Safety Manager

Where are you in your career? Are you just getting by, not rocking the boat, or maybe frustrated that no one is as concerned about safety as you are? That's about how wide across the spectrum that we can sometimes find ourselves, but either way, you swing; you will need to learn how to think out the box and develop strategies to get to where you want and need to be. By now, most of you have experienced the pressures that production management puts on your safety program. In addition, there are many other obstacles, such as dwindling support from senior management, pressures to cut corners, and compromise safety system components that protect your workforce, and ultimately the business.

We need to not overlook attitudes that damage morale and respect and make a commitment to not compromise your convictions. If you are sincere in your attempts to provide a safe work environment, then you will need to investigate emotional intelligence (EI) strategies that will help guide you through many difficult situations…more on EI later in this book.

In conclusion, by the mere fact that you are taking the time to read this book means that you are probably someone who is open-minded and acceptable to new ideas and changes This is my attempt to reach out and share some of my proven concepts that have allowed my safety performance to thrive. Except for one company, I had the challenge to basically start from scratch, building safety programs which has benefited my thinking out-of-the-box approach to safety excellence.

Chapter 3

Assessing Your Program Needs

As stated earlier, the most efficient method to creating your safety program is by determining what hazards your workforce is faced with and attack those issues. Gather the OSHA standards (book) that regulates the type of business that you have. It may be the construction industry or general industry standards, and in most instances, both apply. Get acquainted with the ANSI and NIOSH requirements as well as research what are some of the best safety practices for the industry that your business operates. Join support groups and industry organizations and participate in meetings/gatherings and attend social events to network among others that you may become to rely on for advice...you just may get lucky and find that someone who may be a mentor to you.

After gathering your supporting written materials, physically audit your work task and environment and list all the tools, equipment, machinery, etc. that your workers use and work around to perform their job. Addressing the basics, of course, will be the personal protective equipment (PPE) that needs to be worn to keep their person safe from harm, but remember, PPE is the last line of defense! One tip might be to look at some of the senses that we humans have. What, during the performance of the workers job task, may affect their hearing? How about their breathing or eyesight? Is there a potential risk to contact burns from electrical, chemicals, splatter, or other hazards? Identify the type of clothing a worker must wear and other PPE to protect their head, hands, feet, face, eyes, and hearing.

This project is not only an OSHA requirement to perform a hazard assessment, but it is the requirement that you, the safety professional, have to ensure that your workers are safe while performing job task. Another tip might be to invite your state's occupational safety team to visit your facility to learn from their recommendations. Most state labor departments offer an on-site consultation service. The advantage when inviting state department of labor personnel is that OSHA may give you a pass and take you off their target inspection list if you follow and implement the recommendations that the state team may find to bring your facility into compliance. Their technical advice may surprise you where a fresh set of eyes can, and will, find issues that you may have not thought of or didn't recognize as a hazard.

Chapter 4

Technical Writing

Once you have a good idea of the hazards and risk levels that your workers face, you can start to put it into writing by means of programs, policies, and standard operating procedures (SOPs), as termed *technical writing*. It's the process of detailing how a job task is performed based on regulatory requirements, steps to a task, as well as addressing authorizations, qualifications, and even best practices.

To keep this simple, lets address each separately. The first one will be writing a *program* that is specific to a task or process. A process may include many different tasks to be performed in order to accomplish the job mission. For example, you may have workers operating forklifts at your facility or jobsite, so the written program establishes the requirements that must be followed to become a qualified operator. The *program* may include many safe-operating techniques and the "dos and don'ts" of operation as well as OSHA requirements for training, testing, inspection requirements, and documentation.

The *policy* may detail company-specific information, such as probation periods, performance requirements, rules specific to your company's environment, who can be trained, and when a person is considered competent or authorized to operate equipment or perform certain high-risk task.

The *SOP* may, in detail, show how and what needs to be inspected and instructions that may include information similar to a job hazard assessment (JHA) where steps are identified along with risk and mitigation measures that need to be followed to ensure safe operation.

All these features are considered technical writing, which are specific in details and functions. Just remember, what you put in writing is what you must follow and do. If OSHA investigates any issues and identifies that you failed to follow your own procedures, then there's a good possibility that you will be cited even if OSHA does not have a specific requirement for their finding but will use the General Duty Clause.

You may also reach out to your insurance loss control representatives for copies of generic safety programs that you can use by adding relevant sections to your written plans. It's not necessary to create a document that is solely your own thoughts. Other programs serve as a great resource from companies that have established and proven plans that you may benefit from using. The mark of a great safety professional is not one who knows everything but one who knows where and how to get the information needed and how to apply it correctly.

Just remember, simple is best…as long as the plan covers all requirements and the needs of your workforce to perform their job safely, within acceptable low-risk parameters.

Chapter 5

Implementation Process

In this chapter, I will discuss some of the methods that I have come to use when implementing a new program that my workers needed to know about before performing a new process or task. Be it a single new task or an entirely new safety program, the following steps may serve well for both. After you completed the assessment process and called upon others to assist you and your technical programs are now written...what do you do?

The first step, in my opinion, is the need to assemble senior management as well as project and logistical personnel to review the work that you have completed. They all need to know what you discovered and why it is necessary to implement. Present the information in as much of a professional manner as possible. Most senior management want to see and hear how it affects them and the company. Make sure you do your homework and lay out the information based on regulatory and customer requirements...then address the workers benefits. Most of all, be factual and leave out opinions; your case needs to be bulletproof! Be organized and precise with your intentions, but the ultimate decisions lay with the big boss. There may be some aspects of the safety program that they may have a larger appetite to risk than other parts. This is where you get blocked, which can be most frustrating to the safety manager who is dedicated to doing the right thing! I will discuss this obstacle in a later chapter.

Once your team comes to an agreement, then it's time to publish your technical-writing documents in an easy-to-read format and may be in different languages if you have a multilingual workforce. Use pictures that are specific to your company or industry, making the documents unique to your company!

The next step is to communicate the details to your workforce. This step can be confusing to some, but if conducted in the proper order, it can lend to great benefits to the process. So this step will be broken down into three principal categories: information, knowledge, and experience. (You will notice later in this book that I use this same principle grouping when discussing incident investigations as well.)

- *Information* mainly communicates things that all employees need to know while working at your company. It may include policies, procedures, and SOPs that the workforce needs to be aware of to perform their assigned duties, be it at the company, while on the jobsite at a customers' facility, and maybe traveling between both. This information communication does not qualify any employee to do any high-risk task like equipment operation, working in confined spaces, etc.; this is only basic information that everyone needs to know about.

- *Knowledge*-based communication deals with the training that an employee needs to be offered in order to become qualified and authorized to perform the more high-risk task, such as equipment and machine operator or exposed to risk associated with confined space work, elevated work, electrical and chemical exposures, to name a few, that require detailed training presentations and practical hands-on operation and observations as well as documented testing. This communication principle is required to ensure that the employee gains the knowledge required regarding a specific task or operation. Only after a worker receives knowledge-based communication can a qualification and authorization be granted. With this knowledge-based communication comes more specific rules and regulations and must be retrained if there are any deficiencies noted that the operator may have violated or involved in any incident specific to their qualification.

- *Experience*-based communication is performed when workers have the job experience as an individual or group, like a work crew, and continual information is communicated to all on the crew each day that they work. Such methods used are daily job safety analysis (JSA) before a work shift each day worked. This information is particular to the job being performed and task that are planned to be done that day. It will include equipment to be used, environmental conditions, other contractors at the same site, as well a host of other hazards that the job task entail.

Now that we have reviewed these three communication principles, how do we apply them in an effort to implement your safety plan? I would first address the *information* principle and produce that simple-to-read-and-understand safety manual that contains your management's commitment to safety of its workforce and all the many different programs that you and your team have identified as hazards that are unique to your business. Once produced, publish to all at one time, if possible, so that all employees are made aware of the rules and regulations that are required of them and the expectations to work at your company. The most efficient and beneficial method is through the assembly of your workforce. This gathering of employees gives workers the benefit of asking questions. Each employee should receive a copy of the manual and be required to sign an acknowledgment form that indicates the employee's acceptance of the manual and commitment to follow the contents of the book as a condition of their employment. Thereafter, make this a part of your new-employee orientation process so that all new workers will be informed prior to heading out to a jobsite or a corner in your office building. By providing this awareness information up-front during the hiring process allows your company the best position when dealing with that possible disciplinary situation. This approach is intended to protect both the business and employee alike.

The next step is to ensure that the *knowledge*-based communication is addressed with all workers who are exposed to high-risk task or who operate safety sensitive equipment and machinery. Knowledge communication should be in the form of hands-on training presentations where in-person attendance is required along with participation, specific equipment used, observation while operating, and testing for comprehension. Identify all employees who operate safety-sensitive equipment/machinery or who perform task in or near high-risk environments and schedule training to ensure that all are qualified and authorized to do what they do.

Finally, make sure that your shop-and-field personnel are provided with safety alerts and messages, updates, and specific *experience*-based SOPs, JSAs, and JHAs that will clearly communicate safety-performance requirements. Develop a process to review the in-field JSAs to ensure that the correct information is being used for the proper assignments and risks.

Chapter 6

Training—Empowering for Success

Now I would like to discuss ways that I have come to find very helpful in not only presenting information but also creating buy-in, attention, and interest. When conducting training, I find that starting off with the question of "why" you are here always promotes participation. By discussing this position, you are putting meaning to the presentation and validates the need for the training. Remember, training is a step above awareness and is always specific to the content and situation. Unlike an awareness presentation, training is intended to certify and authorize an employee to perform high-risk tasks, like equipment operation, specific tool use, or working in hazardous environments.

Training content is more than general information shared by all but specific to the high-risk. By getting to the reasons why a person is in your class allows you to create a more personal path to achieving your training mission. Don't, by any means, expect to present required information without meaning. This becomes a lesson in futility and only serves the compliance aspect of your program and lessens the competence of employees trained in ways that spell trouble for their safety down the road. Most accidents occur due to a lack of employee awareness and understanding for the importance of the task being performed. In all interactions, always try to point out the human aspect to safe job performance...let it be your mantra!

Empower your employees with the knowledge that they are the only "one" person who has the best advantage of staying safe at work. Employees need to feel that they are in charge of their actions and always have the right to refuse to perform a task or operate equipment/machinery that they feel is unsafe to do so. They need to feel that their opinion counts and that calling a "stop work" will not result in any negative consequences for them. Encourage reporting unsafe conditions!

Conduct meaningful presentations that are organized and pertinent to the subject matter, including company-specific pictures and videos will make it a more personal experience for all. If you do anything I discuss in this book, don't ever give an answer to a question that you know to be either false or a guess. The best and most credible answer to a subject matter that you do not know the answer is to say "I don't know the answer, but I will find out and get back to you." Portray yourself as a professional and don't do anything that will compromise your credibility. We are not judged by the hundreds of good things we do but rather on the one mistake we make…be mindful and careful to not tarnish your reputation.

Training should be done in person and vetted by providing written test. Test document the training as well as the comprehension of the subject matter. One important element is that the more a business can empower workers so that everyone is talking enthusiastically and knowledgeably about safety issues, the better the results will be.

Chapter 7

Fearless Culture

Safety culture…what does it mean to you? This term has been tossed around for several years now, but many safety professionals I talk to, and management alike, usually describe it right but have no idea of how to systematically improve it. A safety culture is compared to the Latin term "modus operandi," meaning mode of operation in English or MO as we commonly hear it. What is your companies MO? Mode of operation refers to things that are normally done, the characteristics that are unique, like idiosyncrasies.

There is a model that I like to follow that I believe is easy to understand but also presents a clear path to analyzing the current position as well as how to move toward a fearless culture. What do I mean by this? Fearless is where you want to be, but there are several stages in the model that need to be identified and understood before moving forward. In this model, we need to analyze the business capabilities and priorities…and in this following order:

1. Does your business have personnel on staff who have the knowledge and understanding of the risk that your company engages?
2. Do these people have the experience and knowledge to implement mitigation measures, training, and administrative tasks in support of worker safety?

3. Does the business have a written safety program that accurately deals with the risk/hazards that your employees are faced with to perform their task? Are they site-specific?
4. Is there a new-employee safety orientation?
5. Is there a credible and viable training program that address craft, equipment, machinery, etc.?
6. Do employees report unsafe equipment, unsafe conditions, or incidents on a regular basis?
7. Does the business investigate all incidents?
8. Is the information gathered in investigations shared with all employees to include lessons learned?
9. Are there daily prejob safety meetings that are held productively and documented?
10. Are daily inspections performed before starting work?
11. Are workplace hazard assessments performed before work is started each day?
12. Are disciplinary actions taken for safety violations and company policies alike?
13. If your business has a fleet of vehicles, is there a driver's qualification process and maintenance program?

This is my opinion of the top thirteen key-indicators that are a fair measure of a safety culture. As we review each, we start to get a clearer picture of how a business operates regarding the safety of its employees. Of course, there are many more you can add to this list, but for the sake of this exercise, we will use these.

There needs to be competent personnel who can identify and mitigate hazards in the workplace. Without this basic resource, you are running blind! A written and trained program needs to be implemented so that all rules, regulations, and policies are communicated and acknowledged by all employees…it's your guide to doing work safe! Employees have to feel confident (fearless) to report problems as well as to call a stop work if need be. Investigating all incidents thoroughly and communicating lessons learned to all employees is essential to maintaining safe work environments. Holding employees accountable for their actions strikes at the heart of the success of any safety program. OSHA states that if your company does not have a viable disciplinary action process, then you don't have an effective safety program…I agree! Crew leaders need to be taking time before starting work each shift/day to gather all workers and review the task to be performed and any safety related information. Taking care of fleet vehicles and equipment is another essential aspect of any safety program…for this affects not only the workforce but the traveling public as well. Third-party damages can cripple a business!

With this known information, where does your safety culture rank? Are you any of the following?

- Pathological—Your business model is that you don't put much emphasis on any of these thirteen key indicators and only care that you don't get caught. Inexperienced safety support. There are problems waiting to happen.
- Monomania—Only focused on production and complies when need to. Money is a driving factor!
- Reactive—Your business is more reactionary than proactive. There is a belief that it is cheaper to pay the fine than to correct the problems. We don't perform inspections, but we do investigate incidents.
- Enlightened—We know we have problems and are working to improve.
- Proactive—We perform most of the thirteen key indicators, but we still have problems with employees reporting issues.
- Fearless—We perform all the thirteen key indicators and reward employees with incentives when they report issues. We make it a priority to acknowledge reporting and share with all employees ASAP. Employees feel empowered!

This exercise represents my understanding and process that I feel are credible indicators that one can use to analyze the safety culture of their business. If you want a "fearless" safety culture at your business, then be prepared to accept the key indicators as described. Maybe not exactly as I describe but indicators that control compliance and behaviors. These key indicators are called leading indicators because it's a good predictor of performance unlike lagging indicators that only show past performance. It's what are you doing lately that counts! Good luck!

Chapter 8

Good Catch v. Near Miss

In 2008, I was hired as the LIGO safety engineer to oversee the construction activities for an upgrade of advanced technologies to what came to be known as advanced LIGO. Construction activities at the two observatories located in Washington State and Louisiana involved removing older equipment and replacing with new state-of-the art lasers, vacuum system hardware and repairs, computer hardware, optics, seismic isolation, as well as the movement of large and very expensive components. Shortly thereafter, I was recruited to take on the role as the LIGO laboratory chief safety officer, that included R&D Labs located at both Caltech and MIT.

So how do you motivate hundreds of astrophysics scientist, engineers, technicians, as well as a large contingent of third-party millwrights and other support personnel? Many of whom are from different parts of the world with different cultural backgrounds. It seemed that reporting near-misses was a logical step in the right direction but, in my opinion, lacked the proactive component. You see, near-miss reporting only identifies the event that almost caused damages or even an injury but had the potential to at least cause a disruption in the production process. Don't get me wrong, near-miss reporting is a very important tool used to investigate what went wrong or what we could have done differently, but by the grace of good luck, none caused any harm.

Then came the idea to report on findings before they had the chance to cause problems, hence the good catch. The good-catch reporting was communicated to all personnel at the same time and encouraged workers to report to their supervisors even the smallest deficiency or infraction. One may compare this to a behavior-safety practice of the observation and feedback model. The good catch motivates workers to look out for one another and not by just one person at a time walking the floor with a pen and paper recording unsafe acts of others. This model encourages all workers to not ignore a tool laying in the walkway, a sling that is damaged, or even another worker not wearing the proper PPE when required. The final reward was the completion of a $205,000,000-upgrade adventure that lasted over five years (2.9 million man-hours worked), resulting in only two OSHA recordable (medical cases) and a Nobel Prize in Physics. Satisfaction achieved…but what about your situation?

Motivation for LIGO staff came from all the years spent working on undergraduate and doctorate (PhD) degrees, as well as years of research into a passion that they live for. How about the average man or woman working a 9-to-5 job at a dirty and hazardous work site? It's got to be something that piques their interest! Well, money, of course…gift cards handed out for every legitimate good catch reported in a timely manner can be the single motivator for many. When I say legitimate, I mean identifying actions in the mist of tasks or processes. If a worker finds a damaged extension cord while rolling out to their work area one morning is not a good catch…it's called a pre-use inspection. It's the catch while someone using that same cord later and does not notice the damage that may shock them or even electrocute.

Chapter 9

A.C.E.S.©

During the latter years of the 1990s, I was working on my masters in counseling, learning all about personality types, motivation principles, and a whole host of psychology-based topics, as well as behavior biology. I began to think of ways to apply what I was learning to my current profession in safety. I came to realize that some of the tactics that I have relied on and used with success for several years were based in not just theory but reality as well. Well-proven techniques that motivate people and assist in changing the way people perceive things was now going to be the bases of my new challenge of implementing my ideas but seemed to differ from many of the so-called experts in the field of Behavior Based Safety (BBS).

One such tactic that I employed early on in my career was like I just stumbled into it without really knowing what I was doing. It was August 1991, the first day on my new job as the safety director for a power line contractor and reported to work at 0700. As I got out of my car, I noticed a large group of workers standing around in a group, listening to one guy talking. I soon found out that the guy talking and the group standing around were linemen who were protesting the request for an hourly pay raise. It turned out that the power company that we did most of our work for had given their linemen a 1.00/hr. raise, and this group wanted the same. About two months later, I remember visiting a work crew at a local jobsite and saw that same guy who was standing on a crate sharing his grievances with the rest…his name was Merlin.

As I approached Merlin, I commented that I had heard that they received a .50/hr. pay raise. Merlin looked at me kind of sideways and said that he didn't really know because his wife picks up his check each week and he doesn't see it. After hearing what he had said, something hit me like a ton of bricks. I realized that he was the "pied piper" of the crew and that he seemed to be the one person that most looked up to and followed even though it may have not impacted him personally. While visiting the crew, I had some monumental challenges ahead of me due to some noncompliance to safety rules… to say the least. Without going into the details, the gist is that as I befriended Merlin and gained his trust and respect over a couple of months of interaction and conversations, I asked Merlin if he would be willing to help me with the compliance issues. Merlin hesitated a bit but barked off an "okay" and listened to what I had to say. I injected the problem and suggested several solutions, of which he had a choice from. To put in simply, Merlin had the opportunity of individual choice which created an ownership and buy-in to the task at hand. It wasn't long after that the compliance issues were solved which quickly spread to the other work crews. Did I achieve my mission of working with the workers that benefited them the most? You bet! That was the beginning of my long journey to understanding personalities and motivation.

In 1993, I attended a BBS workshop and was having difficulty understanding how do I apply this BBS model to a remote construction workforce that changes work sites on a regular basis… sometimes daily. You see, the premise of the BBS workshop model that was being discussed was mainly based on a captive group of workers, like at a manufacturing facility or auto plant. This environment allows for an ideal situation to group workers into teams and committees that all strive toward the same goals based on the same risk faced each day. The groups play competing games to keep the interest and involvement at a maximum. Workers are scheduled to perform observations of their coworkers (with permission of the one being observed) while on the job and document any unsafe behaviors and counsel them on what they found.

So on the third day, during a break, I approached the well-respected gentleman and asked my question, "How do you apply this model to a remote construction crew working many different sites daily with sometimes rotating personnel?" His answer was, "Have the workers perform observations on each other throughout the day and fix any problems that they find." I was not sure of what he exactly meant, but I was sure that he was not living in my world! I knew that construction workers who perform their jobs at remote sites without the oversight of any management would be a fruitless effort at best to implement such a model. They were just not going to do it, at least not in any credible and consistent manner. Self-perception and responsibility were not typically linked to BBS (Bem 1972) in any meaningful way that would help for the lone or remote worker.

I knew that something was missing, or maybe I just didn't get it. The one thing that I didn't hear, at all, was management's part in all this! Sure, management/supervision coordinated the process, assigning observers their schedule and instructions, as well as little training on understanding the human part of all this. Well, little may not even be accurate due to most not having the background or experience in the understanding of what makes us humans tick. That was my first real experience with the BBS process and never gave it any credibility and knew that there must be a more practical way of achieving employee acceptance to working safe…all the time. There had to be a more realistic way to motivate people to take job safety more seriously.

Near the end of my master's program, I decided that the path I was pursuing with this degree was not of interest to me anymore. I wanted to continue in my safety profession and began to gear my studies and class assignments to a more motivational aspect of my learning. As a result, I created a new (to me anyway) model that would address the whole concept of motivation through facts and example. I knew of all the many different areas of the safety profession that I had to grind through, that most people don't even know exist, were benefiting may understanding of how to better do my job. When you say that you are in safety, most people reply, "Oh…you're that guy that goes around telling people to put their hard hats on, right?"

So I took a leap and came up with A.C.E.S.©, Actively Caring Employers for Safety. This idea grabbed me with such enthusiasm that I found myself thinking about it all the time. After many months of hitting the keypad on my computer, I ended up with about a couple hundred PowerPoint slides…which I thought was pretty good. Well, that changed many times throughout the years following as I realized that I did not know all I needed in order to present A.C.E.S.© in any credible manner that would gain the interest of anyone worth explaining and showing it to. Unfortunately, many businesses are not receptive to new ideas and tend to gravitate toward the more well-known and established programs.

A.C.E.S.© is just not a program…it's not even a process! It's me, David Nolting, and all I learned and experienced over the last thirty-three years in this business of safety management. I have come to realize that A.C.E.S.©, of which I have been building for more than twenty-three years, was a reflection of all I knew…that worked! This concept is based on everything that I write about in this book, its everyone that I have helped, and for all the success that I have achieved. Keeping our workforce safe…every day. It's about thinking out of the box and trying new ways to get the desired results. I know that A.C.E.S.© is a winner because I use it every day, and we are winning. I will explain later in this book but will endeavor to change your outlook toward your safety profession by the time you finished reading it.

In a nutshell, A.C.E.S.© is based on support, motivation, and encouragement by management and supervisors as a company responsibility and the accountability to the workforce. It's like a parent and a child…who raises who? We always hear that the frontline worker is responsible for their own safety and leave it at that. Sure, management presents the training and direction on how to perform their job task, but without a strong commitment and involvement from management, those expectations dwindle. I regard management's participation as safety assurance (S/A), technical writing, job plans, oversight, constant communication, direction, training, support, etc. Safety controls (S/C) are the inspections, audits, PPE, JSAs, visits by management to the work site, to name a few.

The name ACES is not a fancy catchphrase that I wanted to create and promote but rather integrate a concept that is known to identify the willingness to action that we humans have. If I may, I would like to break down this name so that you may learn why ACES is so important to me and why I believe in it as a namesake. Actively describes the actions that must be taken to obtain a desired result. Caring describes the focus that one must maintain when committing to accomplish a certain goal or task. The Employers are the responsible elements to which the outcome relies, while Safety is the objective of all three…Activity, Caring, and Employers. Care is the focal point that drives the entire model to safe work behavior. Employers must understand that what they care about is usually what they put the most conscious energy into, which are displayed in the actions they take. Remember, what we think about all day is what we care about the most. Safety has to be cared about as a core value and must be intergraded into all aspects of the work that the employees are assigned to perform. If safety is not appreciated as a core value, then the actions that management takes will not ensure that the safety of the employees is maintained. The substance of the Care that is focused on, as to the safety of the workforce, will show up in the actions that follow. So addressing the Care aspect must be at the root of the safety culture paradigm change. We need to encourage employers to think differently so that they will act differently and ultimately encourage the workforce to Care for safety differently.

I like to use the term support, rather than enforcement, and that is what A.C.E.S.© provides to the employee. The motivation and encouragement come from showing, in a constructive and empathetic manner, the benefits of sharing safety concerns, thus creating a "fearless safety culture." If the business is truly understood by the safety professional applying A.C.E.S.© to a business, and is presented properly, business owners and management will learn that the benefits far outweigh the cost and time to embrace such a cultural change.

This concept was my way of helping businesses understand what I knew to promote buy-in for the safety of its employees. Managers talk with their frontline supervisors on a daily basis and most of the time about production, schedules, materials, etc., but how often do they discuss safety? Most likely, safety is a scheduled event, like at weekly/monthly meetings, goal setting, and hopefully post incident. A.C.E.S.© is based on continuous involvement and support for workers. A.C.E.S.© directs management/supervision to start off conversations with asking about the safety of the workers… every day. If your program has a system in place that provides for safety alerts and messages as a matter of routine, then management will always have something to discuss regarding safety and obtain feedback.

In my studies and research, I have come to realize that humans are not that much different than other animals when it comes to behavior biology. Lessons learned over the last fifty years have given us a better understanding of ourselves. Years ago, it was thought that the behavior of animals in the wild was for the benefit and good of the pack. Later, more research gathered by zoologist revealed that pack animals displayed a more individualistic behavior and attributed it to protecting their gene lineage for future offspring (Sapolsky 2011). Individualistic behavior is just one of the many biology components that both animals and humans alike share when we interact with one another. Understanding behavior biology allows us to better grasp motivational methods that best fit our needs.

Doctor Sapolsky described in a 2011 class lecture at Stanford University that the basic three elements that animals and humans share are (1) individualism: taking care of the self or self-preservation; (2) selection: what benefits us; and (3) reciprocity: giving and taking, "tit for tat."

There are many more traits that help us to understand behavior, but we will address these three as an example:

- How does a person's *individualism* relate to safety behavior? If we know that humans have the propensity to take care of the self first, then workers need to know what's in it for them personally. Workers need to feel a sense of worth, belonging, and the ability to say when something is wrong or, most importantly, unsafe. They need to have that fearless attitude that speaking up will not always lead to negative consequences but that their voices count!

- *Selection* is important because workers will perform better and follow instructions more closely when they have a say into procedures, policies, and planning. Giving the worker the opportunity to make choices (good ones, of course) helps to create buy-in and acceptance to changes or behaviors in general. Employees are required to follow, without exception, the established rules of a many years ago. Maybe rules laid out by some who really had no credible idea of what they were for or how they apply to the workforce in any practical way. The rules may also be outdated where there are clear contradictions to current times or situations. Allowing involvement promotes and encourages buy-in and acceptance, thus internalizing the decision as beneficial to themselves.

- *Reciprocity* is probably the most important because it deals with trust. Management and supervision must always maintain a trusting relationship with their workforce. Remember in an earlier chapter where I stated that you are not judged by the hundreds of good things you may have done for the workers but rather by the "one" mistake that tarnishers your reputation. Humans have a tendency to use a mistrust incident as an excuse for unsafe behaviors. It's that "they don't care, so why should I" attitude that can be extremely infections among the workforce.

A.C.E.S.© inspires workers to perform at a higher level which ultimately benefits the business and the workers…in many different ways. Workers need support on a continual basis in order to maintain safe behaviors. A.C.E.S.© promotes a direct support system on several levels and not just by a frontline supervisor. Support by management needs to be visual and consistent, with continuous communication, encouraging safe behavior and showing commitment! It needs to resonate throughout the company! I believe that the term "safe behavior" is not only a description for safe work practices but also meaning management's commitment to drive the process. *Managements' behavior is the example set that the workforce will follow.*

Chapter 10

Hazard Reignition Process

In my opinion, hazard reignition is an art! You just can't expect to go out to the jobsite or workshop and capture all the many issues that are either hazardous or has the potential to be. In order to spot a problem, you have to know what you are looking for. Sure, anyone should be able to spot a worker 20 feet above with no fall protection, but if they have a fall harness on, do you know if the worker is trained, tied off correctly, or even wearing the proper companion harness and lanyard? I know that this is low-hanging fruit, but if you expect to become proficient at recognizing hazards, you also need to know how to mitigate them as well.

The following strategy that I discuss is important for anyone who is serious about protecting your workers:

- Do your homework and obtain as much knowledge as possible for the task performed, equipment being used, environments they work in, machinery, tools, etc. Know your risk and hazards!
- Spend time with the workers observing how they work using the tools and such.
- Look for homemade or modified tools…they are not allowed to be used.
- Check for guarding on machines and equipment, electrical cords and outlets (if working outdoors GFCI's are required),

work at heights, around other equipment or objects that pose a struck-by hazard, confined spaces, around chemicals, work in excavations, or any place that the worker can get caught between or engulfed.

- Examine a job setup and identify the "line of fire" hazards!
- List all the many tasks and equipment/tools used and apply the SOPs and programs that you should have in writing, like earlier discussed.
- When approaching a work area, walk the area in different paths…going only one way may limit your field of view. The human eye will only see what it is focused on directly while your peripheral (side) vision does not allow you to recognize details that you are looking for. Medical professionals say that even young people's peripheral vision is poor at best.
- Train others in hazard reignition for a fresh set of eyes. You'll be surprised at how many times I just passed something up when another spotted a problem due to a different angle or interest in a specific hazard that piques their interest more than others.
- Be prepared to LOTO a piece of equipment that you find is unsafe to use or even call a "stop work order"; you have to be deliberate in your actions. Your credibility and the safety of your workforce depends on it!
- Point out to the workers what you spotted as a hazard even if it is adequately controlled.
- Take pictures and audio record your findings and assemble a presentation with all you have found along with corrective actions that were either done at the time of finding or for assignment. Meet with the stakeholders to discuss as soon as you can so that all the issues are fresh to the point.
- You may consult with your legal support to ensure that the materials stay in-house protected by a "client privilege" designation.
- Never leave a *serious or immediately dangerous to life or health (IDLH)* for later correction. Always take action immedi-

ately by applying LOTO or a stop work, if necessary, until the hazard is mitigated and controlled.

- If the hazards identified may be at other locations, communicate them immediately so that all can benefit.
- Train supervisors, foremen, and as many crew personnel as possible on hazard recognition so that all will be able to spot problems.
- Last, but not the least, train your crew leaders in how to perform a workplace hazard assessment and enforce that they are doing before each work shift.

Chapter 11

Investigations

An incident is not always an accident! I hear many people interchange the two but don't really know the difference. According the Merriam-Webster Dictionary, an incident is referred to as "any event or occurrence that takes place." An accident is described as "an unfortunate incident that happens unexpectedly and unintentionally, typically resulting in damage or injury." Now that we are clear on the semantics of these terms, I would like to discuss some ideas that may lessen the stress when investigating both. With any investigation you conduct, I believe that there are three main elements that you must concentrate on to resolve the issues presented. It may be an employee who becomes ill at the job that is not work-related (incident) to the most unfortunate scenario of death (accident) and everything in between.

Remember earlier in chapter 5, on the implantation process, I again will use the same model of information, knowledge, and experience. Let's discuss each in detail and how they apply to your investigation process:

- *Information* is what others tell you about the incident or accident. It's the date and time of occurrence, known damages, and/or injuries sustained. It's the raw data that you will collect as possible evidence that will later be scrutinized for relevance, cause, and effect. Information may come from a wide range of sources, some at the time of your investigation and some way later on down the road. Information allows the investigator to assemble timelines, suspected issues, adding direction going forward. Was company management aware of the unprotected hazards?

- *Knowledge* are the facts that you reveal, like corroborating witness statements, inspection of involved equipment, training logs and certifications, company authorizations, inspection reports, policies and procedures, prior accident investigations that are relevant to your investigation, drug/alcohol testing, etc. These are the elements of the investigation that you can prove to be true or have a better than beyond the "reasonable persons" agreement or understanding.

- *Experience* is all that you and your team possess that resulted in your competency as an investigator—that is, training, how many investigations have you conducted or have been a part of, or your authority to get to the bottom of things. Experience also will come from knowing your risk, hazards, and mitigation measures and how to apply them correctly. These are your skills that you have developed; the ones that sometimes gives you that sixth sense about things because you have seen it before. Your attitude and commitment to find the relevant facts and ultimately the truth. Your experience will help you to fit all the pieces of the puzzle that gives you a clear picture as to what actually occurred and for what reason. Experience and drive can lead you directly to the root cause of incidents or accidents…which is your goal! I liken experience to a person who attempts to put a jigsaw puzzle together with a picture of what the puzzle, when completed, will look like. In contrast to one who attempts to complete one without knowing what it will be, complicating the process.

After compiling all your information, there will come time to complete your written report. This report should be produced on your company or other adopted standard report format. Standardization lends to the credibility of your process. Creating a well-written report will display professionalism and order that will tell your story. Here is an example that you may follow when creating a report format.

The following outline of headings will help you to stay organized and focused:

I. Basic Information
    *   name of investigating organization
    *   date of occurrence
    *   time of occurrence
    *   time notified
    *   location of occurrence
    *   name and title of investigator(s)

II. Overview of Incident/Accident
    *   brief one paragraph of what occurred

III. General Information
    *   description of business operations
    *   names of owners/management
    *   any pertinent information

IV. Description of Incident/Accident
    *   name and contact info of witness(s)
    *   name and contact info of person(s) directly involved
    *   who/what/when/where/how

V. Investigation of Incident/Accident
    *   describe from time you were notified to arrival
    *   what you observed or told upon arrival
    *   the flow of your actions and conversations

VI. Discussion
    *   equipment involved
    *   weather/lighting

- training and experience
- inspections
- policies and procedures reviewed

VII. Root Cause Analysis
- where/whom does the buck stop (I detailed root-cause analysis later in book)

VIII. Conclusion
- lessons learned
- mitigation measures needed
- expectation going forward

IX. Enforcement Actions
- by third-party agencies
- by customer
- by your company

X. Appendix
- persons participating in the investigation
- supporting documentation, evidence, etc.

When following this format, you will need to make sure that your information is consistent throughout. You should only add the facts that are relevant to your investigation, and if you have any theories, back them up with a credible source like your experience or a specific knowledge-based that you possess that directly relates to your investigation and supports your findings. The final report needs to be proofread to ensure that spelling and grammar are correct and that it all makes sense and supports your investigation.

Chapter 12

Correlation v. Causation

In continuation of the previous chapter on investigations, we should look into some of the factors that play a major role into your final decision as to the cause of the incident. I am dedicating a separate chapter on this due to the confusion that we sometimes find ourselves when attempting to inject the pieces of the puzzle into the right places.

Although it is widely quoted that correlation does not mean cause, I disagree and prefer to point out the following. I have read reports where it was not clear to me as to the root cause due to the misunderstanding of the term's correlation and causation. We must understand that these terms are not interchangeable and need to be separate aspects of your investigation focus.

Correlation should be used when referring to those facts that add to the knowledge findings and are pertinent to the possible cause(s). There are the many factors that may have led up to the incident, that without one, like a weak chain link may not have occurred. Such factors may be a failure to inspect equipment before use, not reporting problems, substance-abuse issues, little to no training, etc. that when all accumulated, over time, allowed the incident to occur. Which one was the cause?

Causation, for the sake of my experience, relates to the root cause to what took place. What caused Jim to place himself in harm's way that led to his death? When you look deep enough, you will most likely find that somewhere down the rabbit hole, there was one, or maybe a few, elements of your safety program that were not followed…and could be for more than one reason.

Now that we reviewed the difference between the two terms, let's look at the following hypothetical scenario and discuss the many elements to the event:

> *Jim was a forty-five-year-old worker with five years' experience as a mechanic at the ABC Plant, which is a Rock Crushing facility owned by a heavy highway contractor. At this location, there are several conveyors that move crushed concrete and rock materials around the facility to different locations for separation and stockpiling. Also, there are three front-end loaders that support the movement of materials around the facility. Along the path of the conveyors are crusher bins with mechanical rotating jaws and vibrating presses. On occasion, large chunks of concrete material may get lodged in between the rotating parts, causing a shutdown in operations. There are many other issues that are problematic to this type of operation, but for this scenario, we will use a blockage.*
>
> *On Monday, June 15, 2000, Jim was working on the day shift attending to various maintenance activities on equipment and machinery. At 0920, Jim was called on his radio by the facility manager to come to the number-two crusher for a problem. When Jim arrived at 0923, he met with the manager who advised that the unit stopped operating due to a blockage. At that time, Jim climbed up on top of the number-two crusher bin and jumped in. As Jim was attempting to free the jam, the equipment started up unexpectedly, pulling his right leg into the crusher jaws. When the number-two crusher operator heard the manager screaming, he immediately*

*shut the equipment off. As a result, despite all the
rescue actions taken by other workers at the site, Jim
bleed out and died in the crusher bin.*

As we review this accident, you will note right away (based on
what you read) that there was no lockout/tagout (LOTO) application applied to this event. So many would look at the lack of LOTO
as the cause. Many times, I read reports that say just that! Well, then
why not say that it was the lack of blood that caused Jim's death! A
coroner may list on the autopsy report that Jim succumbed to his
injuries due to a loss of blood, but what caused his death is more
deeply rooted!

The investigation by the regulatory agency concluded the
following:

1. LOTO was not applied and cited the owner a substantial
   fine.
2. There was poor communication between Jim, the facility
   manager, and number-two crusher operator and cited the
   owner a substantial fine.
3. Lack of required LOTO training prior to the accident and
   cited the owner a substantial fine.
4. Operations at crusher facility were suspended for three
   days until training completed and verified to agency.

Investigation completed, training completed and verified, and
$70,000.00 in fines paid. operations resume and all is good! Well,
as it turns out, several key elements were either not uncovered or
just ignored that play a major role into the cause for Jim's untimely
demise.

The following key elements are as follows:

1. There were no hazard assessments performed for this facility that would have documented risks and hazards that
   needed to be mitigated and controlled.

2. There was no site-specific LOTO written plan for the crusher facility.
3. The owner has three satellite sites that equipment and personnel work from for jobs local to their area as well as a main office 40 miles away.
4. The safety manager found on previous visits that workers were entering the crusher bins to unclogged jams similar to the one involving Jim, and no documented actions were taken.
5. On three occasions over the last six months, workers were observed by the facility manager climbing into the crusher bins, and no documented actions were taken.
6. The crusher bins were not treated as a confined space, and there was no written plan at this site.
7. Management did not recognize the confine-space hazard.
8. The crusher facility was not treated as a part of the highway division and had very little oversight or engagement by senior management.
9. Company management addressed safety for highway division more serious due to direct contact with local and state oversight of construction activities.
10. Only three workers at this facility are company personnel; the other eight are hired through a labor contractor and are not included in any company in-house safety training or awareness.
11. Jim was hired five years earlier from this labor contractor and remained on since...not a company employee.

There are many more elements that we can add to this hypothetical scenario, but this is enough! Do we have enough information to decide on a root cause?

Chapter 13

Connecting the Dots—Root Cause

In the previous chapter, we discovered several key elements that were specific to how this highway contractor operates. These elements are like dots that, if connected correctly, may show a more direct cause for Jim's death. You may argue that Jim knew better since he worked at this site for five years…he must have known that the crusher bin was a dangerous place to be in. Maybe so, but it appears that not much emphasis was ever put on this hazard. If we take the eleven key elements that we discovered, we can see that management had little oversight and lacked knowledge or ignored these specific site hazards. Let's look at all eleven elements and see if we can connect the dots based on the safety culture model that we discussed earlier.

#	SAFETY CULTURE QUESTIONS	Yes	No
1	Does your business have personnel on staff who have the knowledge and understanding of the risk that your company engages?		X
2	Do these people have the experience and knowledge to implement mitigation measures, training, and administrative tasks in support of worker safety?		X
3	Does the business have a written safety program that accurately deals with the risk/hazards that your employees are faced with to perform their task? Are they site-specific?		X

4	Is there a new-employee safety orientation?		X
5	Is there a credible and viable training program that address craft, equipment, machinery, etc.?		X
6	Do employees report unsafe equipment, unsafe conditions, or incidents on a regular basis?		X
7	Does the business investigate all incidents?		X
8	Is the information gathered in investigations shared with all employees to include lessons learned?		X
9	Are there daily prejob safety meetings that are held productively and documented?		X
10	Are daily inspections performed before starting work?		X
11	Are workplace hazard assessments performed before work is started each day?		X
12	Are disciplinary actions taken for safety violations and company policies alike?		X
13	If your business has a fleet of vehicles, is there a driver's qualification process and maintenance program?	X	

How does this highway contractor compare to the safety culture model?

- *Pathological*—Your business model is that you don't put much emphasis on any of these thirteen key indicators and only care that you don't get caught. Inexperienced safety support. There are problems waiting to happen.

  ✓ True

- *Monomania*—Only focused on production and complies when need to. Money is a driving factor!

  ✓ We never got deep enough to discover this element.

- *Reactive*—Your business is more reactionary than proactive. There is a belief that it is cheaper to pay the fine than to correct the problems. We don't perform inspections, but we do investigate incidents.

  ✓ True

- *Enlightened*—We know we have problems and are working to improve.

  ✓ No evidence

- *Proactive*—We perform most of the thirteen key indicators, but we still have problems with employees reporting issues.

  ✓ No evidence

- *Fearless*—We perform all the thirteen key indicators and reward employees with incentives when they report issues. We make it a priority to acknowledge reporting and share with all employees ASAP. Employees feel empowered!

  ✓ Not supported by any conclusions or evidence.

After performing this exercise, it should be clear that the safety culture for this company is pathological and that there were indicators that this accident was waiting to happen. After connecting the dots, we find a major root cause as being extremely deficient in awareness, communication, and actions to control workplace hazards for this stand-alone facility. If I were with the agency investigating this accident and discovered these elements, I would be obliged to dig in deeper and interview the owners and senior management, as well as employees on a large scale, to ascertain knowledge and involvement. If senior management knew of their pathology toward their safety culture and did nothing to address it or improve it, then that, my boy, is definitely a root cause to why Jim died at their work site.

Have a system to address all issues and concerns! Stay focused and consistent, and you, too, will discover the hidden pathologies at your business or others out there that you may be a part of.

Chapter 14

Mitigation Methods

Mitigating hazards can be easy or it can be rather difficult, but one tool that you should use is the Safety Hierarchy of Controls Model (NIOSH). This well-known model will assist you in determining what's required to control (mitigate) a certain risk or hazard.

The hierarchy model begins at the top.

- Elimination—Can your operation do without the use of a certain tool, machine, chemical?
- Substitution—Can you use a different, less hazardous chemical or tool?
- Engineering—Add guards to rotating parts, emergency shutoffs, etc.
- Administration—Policies, SOPs, training, signs
- PPE—Hard hats, safety glasses, respirators, earplugs…last line of defense!

I like to use the following scenario when I teach a class on this topic: We, the class, are buying an auto mechanics shop and found a parts washer in the corner of the shop that will come in handy while making repairs. So what I ask the class is to review the Safety Hierarchy of Controls Model and apply the principles to the parts washer as a demonstration into the hazard recognition and mitigation process.

To start, it was identified that the parts washer contained a petro-chemical fluid that is flammable, acidic, and contains many harmful elements that present lung and vital organ hazards. So we as a team explore the hierarchy controls by making the first decision… can we *eliminate* the hazard? We decide that we cannot eliminate because we need the parts washer for cleaning engine parts for repair and reassembly.

So we move on to the *substitution* step and decide that we will use a less harmful citrus-based fluid that is nonflammable with a low risk of acidic exposure and eliminate the risk of harmful fumes and fire hazards.

After making the switch to citrus-based fluids, we assess the entire process and identify that there are other hazards that the worker is exposed to. Lifting heavy parts from the disassembly table to the parts washer exposes risk of back strain and crushed feet if dropped. We also identify that while placing parts into the washer tub, there is a risk of fluid splash as well as while washing the parts themselves. We looked at the *engineering* controls and installed a manual hoist that will assist in lifting heavy parts from the worktable to the washer, which will give the worker a better control of the parts while elim-inating the potential back strains and dropping parts. Mounting a screen made of a clear plexiglass will help prevent splash hazards as well. Additionally, providing ventilation by use of directing any odors away from the worker with a fan. Install adequate lighting that allows the worker to fully see the task he/she is performing.

The team then establish *administrative* controls by writing a standard operating procedure that explains to the worker, the step-by-step process in safely using the parts cleaner. We write a company policy that addresses the qualification and authorization require-ments to use the washer. This may be training requirements, job experience, and responsibilities.

Last, but not the least, we apply *PPE* requirements. Such requirements may be the use of nitrite gloves to protect the hands, splash goggles to protect the eyes, safety toe boots to protect the feet, and require long-sleeved shirts, long pants, and a chemical apron.

Remember…PPE is the last line in defending against hazards they work around!

After performing this exercise, the class gets a clearer insight into how the Safety Hierarchy of Controls Model works and its application process. I also do this for the HAZWOPER training I conduct but on a larger scale and more complicated scenario. The message here is that, if possible, establish a committee to assist in applying these ideas so it is not just your ideas but a team effort which makes for a better possible buy-in by both management and workers, leading to a successful outcome. Don't be weary of your insurance loss control consultants who may be offered as a service. Take the time to foster a respectful relationship that can be extremely beneficial to your success. They can assist you in identifying deficiencies and hazards at your business and, if nurtured right, will help you to get some of the issues solved that you may be trying to implement but are difficult to establish due to management pushback and obstinance. You are both striving for the same outcome…a safe workplace.

Chapter 15

Inspection Process

Your safety program should involve several types and categories that address all known needs for your business. The first step is to develop checklist forms for each of the many areas where work is performed. Checklist may be generic in some cases but may also be specific depending on what's being inspected. There's no good reason why an equipment operator should be filling out an inspection checklist for an office environment. The point here is be specific to the risk/hazards that are associated with the inspection.

An inspection is a formal way to collect information using the forms that you develop for the area(s) that need to be inspected. The forms should be specific with questions that guide the inspector through the process. Inspections are usually conducted in two ways, impromptu and scheduled. Information collected by the inspector may also include photographs, video, or even audio recordings.

Impromptu inspections are not usually announced and are designed to observe the workers in action as well as while on breaks or gone for the day. Why unannounced? Because unlike a scheduled inspection, workers will not have the opportunity to hide unsafe behaviors, tools, equipment, etc., like when they are expecting you. You get a chance to observe housekeeping, and also, arriving during a break can help you better understand what the workers are doing.

I remember conducting a quarterly safety audit at a shipyard facility that was announced weeks in advance, and the workforce knew I was coming. Halfway through the inspection I was observing a pretty-organized work environment with proper PPE, fall protection, guarding, etc., but when the midmorning break came, and the workers put down their tools and went to the break area, I was seeing through their smoke screen. Several workers left their oxy/acetylene torches in confined space areas. Although the gas was shut off at the torch, the hoses remined charged with oxygen and flammable gas. This is a serious issue for confined-space work and gave me more insight as to what was really going on. After the workers returned, I ordered a stop work and addressed the issue right there. As it turned out, the workers didn't recognize the area as a confined space because it was not following the typical definition…but still provided a confined space for hot-work activities. A leaking torch can lead to catastrophic consequences when squeezing a striker to light the torch with several cubic feet of oxy/acetylene gas present.

A scheduled inspection is usually performed on a monthly, quarterly, or even on an annual basis. It all depends on what your mission is. Are you following up on a new process or machine that was added to the shop? Maybe an annual inspection by your insurance loss prevention representative or a remote work crew that you don't see much.

Another inspection form that I developed was for a field crew that was working a job at a surface mine in the Midwest and was having problems controlling minor safety issues at the site. I went out for a visit to find out what was happening and identified the need to help the crew engage safety in a more organized way. As it turned out, the crew were inspecting their tools and equipment before use each morning, and a JSA was performed, but only a couple of the crew were actively engaged. So I developed a Daily Site Safety Activity Report (checklist) of all the areas that were being overlooked throughout the day that the customer's safety folks were finding. This checklist was to be completed in the morning as work was beginning and after returning back from lunch break. The checklist was reviewed with all fourteen crew members, explaining how each item was to be inspected and was to be performed by a different person each day. Again, an inspection checklist specific to the job task and environment.

Just as we discussed in the chapter on hazard reignition, you have to be methodical in your approach. If you are the only one doing the inspection, walk different paths and stop to ask questions. The inspection process should not be just to find issues that are unsafe but to interact with the workers to establish an understanding as to what you are doing and how it benefits them personally. Engage and compliment good findings.

Chapter 16

Prevention through Design

Prevention through design is the concept of addressing safety risk and mitigating hazards during the design process before a structure or piece of equipment is built. To some of you, this concept is irrelevant to the safety work that you do, but for others, especially safety engineers, this is the bases for their work. Some safety professionals may never get the opportunity to be included at the design phase, and oftentimes, you wish you had. If you work in this profession long enough, there will be a time that your wish may come true.

After managing the safety for a few high-hazard construction companies, I had the opportunity to work at LIGO and was first hired as the project safety engineer. Was I an engineer…did I have an engineering degree…no! But what I did have was a master's degree and nineteen years' experience at those high-hazard construction companies. The $210M project funded by the National Science Foundation (NSF) called for construction experience, technical writing, and analytical skills, of which I had all three. During the first three years, I worked closely with the design engineers, technicians, and scientist developing assembly and installation hazard analysis. The process was consistent across all the many dozens and dozens of hazard analysis review meetings and was accomplished by applying the principles outlined in the adopted system installation hazard assessment. The outline headings were as follows:

1. Summary
   - overview with table identifying hazard-risk assessment levels and number of hazards associated with the installation processes
2. Forward
   - list potential hazards to a specific component for installation and operation and reference documents
3. Introduction
   - brief description of component
4. Hazard Identification and Assessment
   - with table of hazard severity categories, hazard levels, risk-assessment matrix, and risk code criteria
5. Hazard Analysis for Standard Operations
   - hazards—that is, electrical, eye, hand/finger, etc., with mitigated risk assessment levels identified

The hazard assessment completed documents ran anywhere from twenty to thirty-five pages in length and detailed all concerns, especially those that were brought up by me doing the process. In effect, I had control of the final product and remained in the loop throughout. The final stage was a formal sign-off process that required all management principles signature before being published. Although working under the oversight of the NSF and scientist from both Caltech and MIT, there were still some tense moments involving issues that required an experienced construction safety professional to solve.

As an example, to some of the safety design-in processes was the in-house design and manufacture of an apparatus that was used to install optics (mirrors) that were ~16 inches in diameter by ~10 inches wide. The optics weighed ~70lbs at a cost of ~$250,000.00 each. This apparatus named the Ergo Arm had a vacuum device attached that sucked into the optic as an attachment as it was precisely installed. The Ergo Arm was a one of a kind and mitigated the risk of injury and damages. There were several other developments such as this and went on to serve the assembly and installation activities very well…no damages or injuries as a result to careful planning and execution.

Other design-in safety features may be the installation of railings and anchor points at time of manufacture, providing a safety measure for workers to utilize during construction and assembly activities. There are many examples of adding safety features at the design phase and play a vital role in preventing worker incidents, such as lighting, ventilation, anchor points for fall-arrest equipment to name a few more. The basic intention is to design safety features into the job of assembly, erection, and for future maintenance activities that mitigate risk to the workers or processes. Downstream protection!

Chapter 17

Risk Management Process in Construction

Now that you have managed to read through all my suggestions and opinions, I would like to discuss some of the risk management strategies that I have applied over the years that I feel will be beneficial to you, the reader. When we think of risk management, many think of risk appetite…how much are you willing to chew off or swallow as part of your business plan? But when it comes to the safety of our employees, there *is* no appetite! So right there, we see the difference between worker safety and risk management. Some may disagree with this statement, but for me, I am all in on this ideology. In this chapter, I will discuss risk-management applications in the construction environment only.

Let's not confuse a risk for a hazard…they are two different terms that are consistently used when managing your safety program. To clarify, hazards are those sources that present a direct potential of unavoidable harm to people, property, equipment, and the environment…even if we know about it in advance. A risk is the level of potential harm that may occur if affected by the hazard. The risk analysis reviews the hazard for its potential harm and apply mitigation measures to eliminate the hazard or mitigate to an acceptable level that protects the worker and the environment. I feel that there are two different types of risk: internal risk and external risk. The internal risks deal with the culture of the business or safety program. As described earlier, there are many issues that a business can control that are directly attributed to the attitude of the business culture. If business and safety management are in agreement with the Fearless Safety Culture attitude, then half the battle is won or maybe adequately controlled. Too often we are our own worst enemy when our risk appetite gets too big and we ignore the possibilities of the external risk. External risks are those issues that have to be evaluated and assumptions made to maintain a viable risk management strategy that protects the worker and the business. Such assumptions that anticipate obstacles and roadblocks that are possible and proper planning that deals with the event or situation. Contingency planning is just as important as the initial plan itself. The key to this stagey is to qualify the assumptions and to review occasionally to ensure accuracy. As I stated earlier, a Plan B is always needed because Plan A is sometimes the first casualty of battle.

Risk management in construction is a methodical process that requires knowledge and understanding for a wide variety of situations; some involving survey and testing applications as well as strict management challenges that are designed to control and manage risk that are both known and unknown to the work that we do. I will review for the reader two real-life scenarios that I was directly involved in that was worth all the efforts put into it. Although many or most may not share my experiences, this is intended to help you to think out of the box for your specific needs.

The first risk management strategy involved performing air and dust sampling for a hopper barge cleaning operation that had just off-loaded a cargo of lead ingots. The transportation of lead ingots via way of waterway hopper barges was another revenue stream that the company I was working with, as the safety supervisor, was attempting to engage in. When I first found out about this, I inquired into the method of packaging etc. and learned that the ingots would be palletized around four feet tall, with the ingots being the size of common house building bricks or maybe a little larger. The ingots would be secured to the pallets by metal straps, with no covering. I won't go through all the conversations I had with sales staff and management but will share the strategy and application that I decided needed to be done to protect my workers. The attitude among management was that there seemed to be no safety issues since the lead ingots were no different than that a fisherman handles as a weight on their lines. I had a different opinion and assembled a plan of action to test my theory that the handling of lead was goanna be harmful to the health of the workers and needed to be investigated.

By this time with this company, I had been through a formal training program and was certified as an industrial hygiene technician...not hygienist! I was trained in the understanding and application into the use of air, water, noise, particle sampling equipment and its ways of use. The plan involved specific training for the five workers selected and suiting them up in Tyvek coveralls, respirators, nitrite gloves, boots, and splash-proof goggles. Each worker wore a monitor, sampling the air in their berating area, as well as a few monitors stationed at dedicated points of the cleaning operation. After the cleaning operations were completed, the air monitors and cartages were sent to a local lab to be analyzed, as well as two particle/dust samples (2 pints) of a container of ~55 gallons of dust that was collected as a result of push-broom cleaning activities.

This exercise revealed that the lab analysis showed a very high concentration of airborne lead particles that pose extreme risk to the workers' health. In addition, the dust particle ground samples, when analyzed, also showed a very high concentration of lead in the dust, which meant that the ~55-gallon container was now considered as a hazardous waste product and required by LADEQ to be discarded in a strict and specific manner...expensive!

The formal report that I submitted to management, which included the analytical evidence, became the decision maker to not seek the lead ingot transportation business. The key decision was not really the health of the workers but rather the very high cost involved when you are talking about cleaning a barge (200' × 35') that was previously loaded with lead ingots by using water. The thousands of gallons required to properly clean a hopper barge would in effect become a hazardous waste. Disposal cost would far outweigh the profits made. Worker's safety maintained...mission accomplished!

The second strategy was designed to protect both the workers and the motoring public for a major interstate roadway project that spanned 14 miles in both east and west bound lanes, including on/off-ramp interchanges.

I was charged with the design, implementation, and oversight of an in-house financed Motorist Assistance Patrol Program (MAPP) that would be specific to this project. This highway model of assistance did not exist at the time that this occurred and is now mostly handled by states DOTD throughout the nation. We equipped two F-250 pickups with all the required tools to assist vehicle breakdown and accidents in the construction zone. Included was a two-way communication system with local and state police/fire as well as project management personnel. We hired a retired police officer and off-duty firefighters to operate the MAPP vehicles. These off-duty firemen not only had experience in emergency services but were also trained as first responders which greatly increased the effectiveness of on-site medical care for injury incidents. They worked two twelve-hour shifts.

Also, a video camera was mounted on the dashboards to record the work zone before work started each day as well at the end of the MAPP work shift. The video captured the placement of traffic-control devices that were strategically placed based on the Manual on Uniform Traffic Control Devices (MUTCD) for streets and highways that was specifically designed for this project. The correct placement and maintenance of the traffic-control devices is a critical aspect in the risk management of the construction project and for the safety of all on-site working and citizens driving through daily. In addition, a team was assembled that included insurance claims, attorneys, expert accident reconstructionist, and medical-care facilities. This team was charged with the responsibility to manage third-party incidents that rose to the level of moderate to major.

I met with local and state emergency management committees to discuss our MAPP initiative as well as project dynamics. The MAPP gained the attention of the Federal Highway Commission who solicited our feedback for the MAPP process, effectiveness, and opinions to better manage the safety of highway work zones.

As a result of the MAPP being a total success in managing the risk to the project and public, we received the Louisiana's annual

"Total Commitment to Public Safety Award" presented by the governor.

These are the two examples of construction risk management with the emphasis on protecting human life and not playing the risk-appetite game.

Chapter 18

Job Hazard Assessment (JHA)

Job hazard assessments are used to identify risk and hazards that may be present in a particular work environment or what potential safety issues might develop. I like to use JHAs to address site-specific safety issues as well as a training tool and awareness education for all workers.

Without going through all the details, there are four main elements that you need to identify and address in this process:

1. What are you doing or plan to do?
2. What are the risks or hazards associated with the work environment or with the work you are planning as well as the possible negative impacts that may occur to people, property, equipment, or the environment?
3. What are the mitigation or control measures required to prevent injury or damages?
4. Who is responsible and accountable to ensure that the mitigation or control measures are followed?

These four elements are followed through in a step fashion from the beginning of the activity and throughout—that is, number 1 to number 8 or more steps depending on the dynamics of the task or activity. They shall include task, equipment/machinery being used, tools, rigging, etc. A JHA is similar to the job hazard analysis that

I write about in chapter 16, "Prevention Through Design," and is intended to establish mitigation and control measures to prevent injury or damages. The differences are that this job hazard assessment is mainly specific to the jobsite environment and intended to establish a site-specific safety plan and arguments the daily job safety analysis (JSA) that I write about in the next chapter. As you will read in the next chapter, job hazard assessments are developed for two main purposes. First, to identify the major risk and hazards for the jobsite and second, to argument the daily job safety analysis as a reference document.

I realize that the acronym "JHA" for both job hazard assessment and job hazard analysis can seem confusing, but the last word in each should explain the difference. JH analysis, in my opinion, is used to preplan for the hazard and risk dynamics, and the JH assessment is a final pre-build document…the anticipated exposures.

Chapter 19

Job Safety Analysis (JSA)

The job safety analysis (JSA) is commonly used during a daily job briefing or tailgate meeting prior to starting work each shift or workday. The JSA details the work that is planned for that upcoming shift or workday. JSAs can change from day to day depending on work activities and can sometimes be pretty much the same for longer periods of time when task do not change. But just because the task may not change, the environmental conditions may change that could interfere with the safe operation of equipment and tools.

I can remember a time early in my safety career when using daily toolbox talks were the norm. Unfortunately, toolbox talks are mostly specific to one topic and were marketed as the ten-minute safety meeting. This gave a sense of security that you were doing the right thing and having it documented as well. These ten-minute talks really didn't make much of difference but was better than nothing… at least the crew met before starting work. The JSA that is now commonly used evolved into a 20–30-minute safety meeting as well as a good time to ensure that your workforce is fit for duty that work shift or day.

The JSA details jobsite information, date, any PPE or special safety equipment to be used, inspections, environmental conditions, as well a description of the upcoming work plan activities. In addition, all workers are to sign the JSA form documenting their attendance. In an effort to prevent pencil-whipping the JSA form, I assign numbers to my JH assessments so the person completing the form can write in the corresponding JHA number to argument the JSA process. The JH assessments are kept in a job folder at the site along with blank JSA forms. The JH assessments should be readily available at the time of giving the JSA as a reference to address the specific safety hazards and risk for that day or shift.

One tip that you might want to add to your JSA form is to not only require all attendees to sign the form before the meeting starts but also include a place for them to put their initials at the end of the work shift that indicates that they did not sustain any injuries or illness while at that the jobsite that workday. By adding this feature to the form, it allows you to better control injuries either legit or not.

Chapter 20

Thinking "Out of the Box"

We sometimes find ourselves kneeling to the "status quo" when it comes to some of the challenges we come up against. Examples may be capitulating to managements pushback on certain safety rules to allow production to press on. Another might be when attempting to apply training for a new tool or task with a method to mitigate a hazardous situation or perceived risk and no one is in support or gives lame excuses.

One such time, I can remember introducing a "Lift Plan Worksheet" to our supervisors to review and try to complete, which would provide important and useful information regarding safe load handling with skid steers at their work sites. This worksheet was intended to be completed before work was started at a new project. The reason is mainly not for what we pick up, which is the same load weights at most jobs, but because we rent the skid steers, and this would enable the crew to make sure that the equipment rented was capable of the load lifts and safe movement around the jobsite. Within hours, I received some feedback from one of the project managers indicating the need to discuss. After a few days, the project managers and I attended a scheduled planning meeting, and this topic was raised for discussion. The belief of some of the project managers was that by completing this worksheet, we might be putting ourselves in a jam with our customers if we did not follow the safe requirements detailed in the worksheet.

So I asked the one question, "If we have an incident involving a skid steer carrying a load and someone ask how much the load weighed and the capacity of the skid steer, what's the answer?" It was obvious to me that this group did not understand that they, at this time, were putting themselves in legal jeopardy if in the event that an incident did occur with one of the skid steers sometime in the future. I stood my ground and added that the reason for the worksheet was to solicit a conversation that would eventually get us to that point. The point being was that now everyone was aware of the issue as well as managements responsibility to the workforce.

It wasn't too long after that meeting that another local contractor had an accident at their site involving a skid steer moving a load with the attached forks. It was revealed that the operator did not know how much the load weighed or did he know the safe-load rating limits for the equipment he was operating. *Wala*...plan accepted and implemented across the board. In this example that actually occurred, you sometimes need to strategize and figure out the right time to get your plans accepted.

I know that many readers may say that they would just push back and implement the plan, but sometimes, it's not that simple. This book is intended to help safety managers who don't have a solid support system at their company unlike most large businesses who employ a team of safety professionals to handle safety management task. But even those so-called large companies sometimes become masters at cutting corners! If you are a person who just goes with the flow and are comfortable not making any waves, then you probably should resign your position because you are not doing any one, employer or employee, any good. But if you are that safety manager who knows things could, and should be better, then you need to learn how to think out of the box. Challenge yourself to conquer managements' obstinance and figure out ways to give them what they need. This is the best reason to have a mentor who you can bounce issues off and help you to make the decisions that compliment your convictions and goals.

Another great tip for thinking out of the box is to study business strategies that are well-recognized and used at many top companies around the world. Such as the "law of diffusion" when attempting to roll out a new program to solicit the correct group within your company that statistically will most likely share buy-in first or who are most likely the early adaptors. Read up on "shifting baseline syndrome" which shows that if something is consistently repeated, it changes ideas as an acceptable new normal or way to do things. If you can change a worker's mind on safety, then their actions will follow.

A very successful strategy deployed back in the 1990s was the "Broken Window Project" in New York City. Simply put small and often overlooked housekeeping issues in neighborhoods became the center of concern for policing, which ultimately led to better communication in the communities with the police as well as evolving into a closer partnership. As the small issues were addressed, the larger crimes diminished. Do yourself a favor and read up on this theory put into a reality project that changed New York City for the best.

In conclusion, written safety rules and regulations are not going to propel your safety program to the next level you might strive for all by themselves. It is for this reason alone that it requires the safety manager to think out of the box to create an advantage that benefits both the company and the workforce. Advantages that separate your safety program from others, being a leader for innovations and not just following the status-quo. I once heard that there are only two ways to survive; think like a fox and avoid the traps or act like a lion and scare away your enemies! Well, I think that using a little of both, smarts and action, can be utilized to overcome obstacles and obstinance. Use whatever it takes to ensure the safety of those you are charged to protect. Everything I've done through most of my safety career has been influenced by my ambition to be different. I realized early on that I wanted to make a difference and had the confidence to do so!

Remember, the most dangerous phrase in safety is "we've always done it that way."

Chapter 21

Raising the Bar

As we discussed in the previous chapter, if you want to create separation value, you need to raise the bar on safety performance by thinking out of the box. Raising the bar on safety performance does not just mean achieving safety compliance but rather on how you go about doing it. It's like comparing lagging indicators to leading indicators. One describes what you were and where you have been, and the other shows where you are headed and how you are planning to get there. When I audit a program, I am mostly concerned with the leading indicators, which are good predictors for success, showing commitment and actions.

Building on your leading indicators that address goals and performance will point you in the right direction but needs to be established in parallel to your business model. Most business models are finite or infinite. Each one tends to operate within common boundaries with one another, but that's where it ends. If your business is characterized as *finite*, then you tend to only do what's necessary to make a profit, whereas an *infinite* model goes beyond the necessary and strives to be an innovator and has the best chance to survive and outpace the finite. The infinite model employs strategies that attempts to separate themselves from the competition and encourages employee buy-in and ownership into what they are hired to do for the business. This infinite model also is where you find that true safety can be realized. So in order to raise the bar in any realistic and functional manner, the business needs to decide if the bar can be raised and if they have the will to do it.

In my experience, raising the bar means going beyond the necessary and establishing safety mitigation that goes steps above what the regulatory agencies require. Safety managers are the ones who know what's best to achieve safety, and it's for that reason that we need to be smart and aggressive to get us there.

As I explained earlier, my attempt to raise the bar was realized through the creation of A.C.E.S.©. This process allowed me to formulate a plan of action that was organized and consistent with the business model I was working with. My mission with A.C.E.S. is to create a paradigm shift that changes the way safety professionals go about protecting their workers.

Creativity and innovations come from identifying ideas that can separate your safety program in ways that allow you to establish credibility and respect by your peer organizations and customer base. Listing ideas that you may come up with don't need to be all inspiring and ready to implement. Ideas need to be nurtured in ways that keep them in the shadows and viable to spotlight at the right time. What I mean by this is that some ideas may not be practical at the moment, but building on them throughout time can evolve into a significant advantage down the road. I cannot tell you how many ideas I had that were not developed but keeping them in the back of my mind, meshed with other ideas that were implemented with positive impacts. As I discussed earlier, the implementation of the MAPP realized an extremely positive impact and was only an idea and vision when first talked about.

As Albert Einstein once stated, "Imagination is more important than knowledge. For knowledge is limited to all we know and understand while imagination embraces the entire world and all there ever will be to know and understand."

Chapter 22

Be a Leader...Not Just a Manager

Throughout this book, the theme is that you have to be different if you want to make a difference! Making a difference requires great leadership and not just good. Great leaders display ambition to drive the safety program to higher levels while inspiring management and workers to be their best. Motivation through empathy is a key element to succeeding as well as employing emotional intelligence traits that develop trust and acceptance to what you are trying to accomplish. Great leaders will have a plan A as well as a plan B. We know through history that many times, war strategy always has a plan B… because plan A is most always the first casualty of battle. Plan your actions accordingly and develop fallback options.

Great leaders have vision that guide them through change. It's not being a friendly person that gains you respect but the fairness and consistency that creates trust and respect. Great leaders know how to hold workers accountable by using clear expectations and communication. They know how to inject emotional intelligence into their role as leader as well as internalizing emotions that may distract the performance of others. Workers will follow strong personalities that they trust as long as honesty is shown in a fair and consistent manner. Being a great leader challenges others to be and do their best at their task. Great leaders were probably great followers at one time; they knew how to accomplish their goals while helping others with theirs at the same time. These leaders have vision that allows them to see five moves ahead, anticipating problems and solutions on the go.

Managers basically steer the business throughout the processes where leaders move the business forward. Great leaders are the ones who see the future and maneuver through a path to higher standards and reputation. Great leaders can be counted on to do what's necessary and can be depended on during critical times. Growth is their goal, and change are their actions. If you want to be a great leader and not just a manager of your safety program, then be inspired to look within yourself and decide if you are that person. Take on additional task and assist your boss to make them better at what they do. Eventually, you will be the boss!

Being a leader is not a position, it's a trait that not all can obtain. There are many leaders who are not managers, and there are many managers who are not leaders. The one thing for sure is that there are not many leaders without egos…those are called great leaders.

Chapter 23

Emotional Intelligence

This chapter on emotional intelligence (EI) is probably the most import part of this book. Without this skill, most people never realize their potential...and never knowing why. It was once thought that a person's intelligence quotient (IQ) was a great predictor of one's possible success in life and business. Having a high IQ and being intelligent was going to lead you through life's journey to success, allowing you to aspire to anything that you wanted to be. There are many people with advanced degrees and higher than the average IQ who do very well in life and in their career fields, but take them out of their bubble and hand them the responsibility of managing people and most fail miserably.

Just because a person has a high IQ does not make them a candidate to become a leader or even a manager. To be a good manager or leader, you have to understand who you are as well as those you interact with and who depends on you. It's knowing and accepting who you are, with all your faults and strengths. Self-reflection and identifying what you project to others is the first step to EI. You must be able to regulate your demeanor and actions so as to not relate your thoughts into actions in unintended or unproductive ways. You need to think before talking sometimes so that your intentions inspire your actions. An example might be during a tense moment with someone where you are angry or disappointed and just want to say what's on your mind. But managers do not have the privilege to just say or do what they want; they must react with a sound posture that de-escalates the issue and stives to resolve problems that are germane to the event or situation. We must learn to put our egos aside for the betterment of the position you are in. If you think you are open and accessible and your team doesn't think so, then you have a problem. Your perception of yourself must be based in the reality of what others see and hear.

In an earlier chapter, I discussed the fearless safety culture and what it means to your safety program. Emotional intelligence plays a major role in this culture model where you must put aside your ego and let others inject their ideas and concerns…or feedback as we call it. We need feedback and responses that are productive, thus paving a way for trust and growth. This is where creativity is spawned and innovations are born. If you are passionate about your mission or goals, then display that passion to your workers. Help them to understand that your safety program is not just about rules and regulations but about them and their families. Pass on this infectious feeling to others so that they can feel what you do. If you are a person who sits behind your desk all day reading reports and sending emails, then you need to get out in the field or shop and get "down in the hole." Help, assist, explain, show what they need to feel to make them safe. When you do this, you will motivate others to do or be better, which can lead to developing future supervisors and managers.

The second important element of EI is to understand people. You need to understand that not everyone has the same personality, cultural ideologies, experiences, motivations, or even goals in life. It's for these few reasons alone that you must study human emotions and tendencies so that you can understand what motivates some and not others. Understanding what makes others tick will better help you to plan a strategy that works for most. When I say "most," I don't mean everyone. There are always going to be some who don't care, for various reasons, but identifying some ahead of time can help you when choosing teams.

The third element of EI is to learn how to interact in constructive and productive ways that achieve your goals and mission. Study body language queues and learn how people communicate their feelings and intentions as well as your own. Communication is probably one of the most difficult things that we humans do. It can easily be misinterpreted in many ways, so we need to make sure that what we mean to say or do is perceived the way you intend it to be. There are several tips on communication, but for the most part, clarification is the easiest. Clarification is accomplished simply by stating your intentions and then ask the person to tell you what you said back then reaffirm if it was correct. This communication strategy is most common when asking someone to perform a task at work. If done professionally and correct, then there should be no misunderstanding of your intentions and expectations. You can see here how this plays a major role when it comes to a safety-sensitive situation where lives are at risk.

Educate yourself on the dynamics of EI and incorporate them into your training and interactions in your work setting...or even your social and personal life. Take classes, read the books and literature, as well as attend workshops on the topic. Once you have a grasp of EI, then plan to educate your supervisors and project managers on this skill set. Solicit all at the company who interacts with the workforce. People feel safe when they see that their boss is taking safety at the company serious and in a consistent manner. The only way that we can help the workforce see and feel this is by knowing how to show it. Remember, your mind has to be stronger than your feelings. The emotionally intelligent leader frames everything from the point of view of his or her team, by communicating what the opportunity means for everyone together, what it means for individual contributors, and what's specifically needed from each person to reach the stated goal.

My masters in counseling afforded me the opportunity to formally learn and practice the traits of human behavior and all the dynamics that make us tick. This was definitely an edge for me!

Chapter 24

Understanding Your Customers

Most in the safety profession would assume that your customers are your workers and management that you are charged to protect as the company safety manager, but in this chapter, I would like to discuss the customers that your company does business with. There needs to be a balance of respect and professionalism that helps sustain your relationship with customers.

When dealing with customers, it is important that you put your best foot forward and be prepared for any and all challenges. When I send a crew to do work for a new customer, I make sure that all the Is are dotted and the Ts are crossed. I make contact with the site safety manager or their boss if available to create a relationship that opens a line of communication that shows commitment to safe work practices at their facility. It's better to have this established in advance before any issues occur that puts you on your heels.

My mantra is that we will go to work prepared to be the best at what we do and the safest client that they have. My intention is to put the customer on their heels and don't give any room to complain. Remember, you are dealing with personalities, and how you handle depends on your emotional intelligence. All required safety documentation is established as well as a site safety plan detailing what we will be doing as well as certifications for equipment operators, rigging, safety data sheets, training, inspections, JSAs, etc., on our company forms. Providing quality and organized documentation with company logo will go a long way when first arriving at a new site. If done right, you may be providing more quality safety documentation than the customer may have for their own company. If the customer is one that has several facilities in different states, then introduce yourself to the corporate safety professional or the person at the top of the safety ladder. Always have, if possible, a go-to safety person to help rectify any safety-related issues or concerns that may arise from the site you are working. What do I mean by this statement?

On occasion, you might find that the site safety manager may seem to be targeting your workers in a way that reveals a nitpicking array of constant little things that never seem to end. Of course, if your workers are using unsafe tools or equipment or performing in unsafe ways, then that is a different story. But when site safety sits back taking pictures of perceived safety issues and sending to their management team as an "I gotcha" moment, without first addressing the issue with you or your workforce, can be a problem.

I experienced just this scenario at a project and, after calling on the corporate safety director to discuss, learned that the site safety manager was having a difficult time with safety compliance within their own company and out of frustration leaned on us to compensate for their worthiness. I have also experienced site safety climbing the company ladder and was trying to make a name for themselves. Unfortunately for them, their tactics were off base and rooted in opinion and not in best practice or regulatory mandates. For example, a site safety person told our crew that they did not need to wear a face shield for the angle grinder they were using because they were only buffing the material and not grinding. Well, when using a hand-angle grinder operating at ~12,000 rpm, what's the difference when any type disk pad fails and flies apart? I don't know what he was thinking, but we continued to wear face shields. Pick your battles accordingly and don't make it your mission to prove someone like this person wrong. Emotional intelligence will help you deal with issues like this and will benefit you and your company in the long run.

Chapter 25

Produce a Professional Product

The product you produce will be a reflection of your company and ultimately of you as the safety professional. This perception will be looked upon by your customers, your peers, regulatory agencies, as well as anyone who you interact within the realm of safety management. Develop a systematic approach to your safety program and produce quality documents that follow the same format and style in an organized manner. Track all incidents and accidents, recognizing trends and causal relationships. Provide clear and pertinent information for training presentations and documents.

Packaging your product is also important when presenting to customers or other requesting entities. Assemble in an easy-to-find-and-read format, displaying a snapshot of your safety program. The following Safety Program Tree is an example of how I present my safety program in its entirety at a one-glance presentation.

SAFETY PROGRAM MANAGEMENT

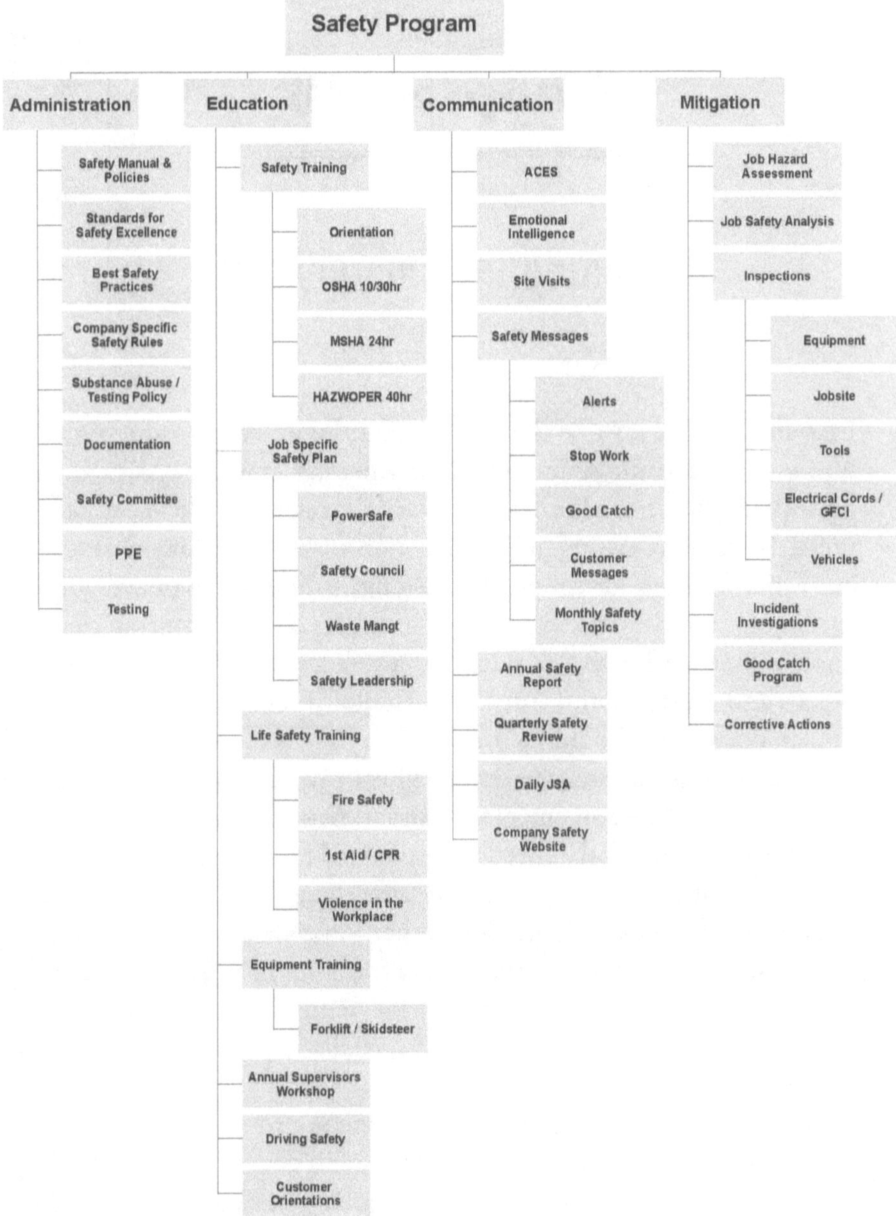

Chapter 26

Planning for Emergencies

Last, but not the least, is the need to plan for emergency situations. As we all should know by now, that when an emergency situation presents itself, we are limited in our choice as to how to deal with them. If we don't create an escape action plan in the case of fire at our office building or shops, then we limit the actions to everyone fending for themselves. So identifying exit routes and ensuring clear, unobstructed pathways is a start, but awareness exercises with alarm signals and muster points must be included. This is a simple plan to implement and so should be the rest that you, as the safety manager, must identify as necessary to ensure all your workers are afforded the best advantage when an emergency situation occurs.

Other situations that need to be planned for are extreme weather events, fire of many types that may affect your locations, chemical release, floods, active shooter and other violence in the workplace, gas leaks, power outages, over-the-road travel support, business interruption, and injury and illness management. There may be many more that you may discover and are specific to your operation and location.

Again, select members of your company to help in this process and develop easy-to-read-and-understand documents that detail company policy and action requirements. Finally, conduct awareness education meetings that explain the plan and practice evacuations to include alarms and muster points. This may also be a good time to implement a first aid/CPR/AED training to include as many employees as possible to ensure that there is adequate assistance available at all times in case of that emergency situation.

Proper planning will increase the probability that your workers will survive most emergencies that occur. With repartition and support, the choices made will be the right ones for the situation presented.

Conclusion

As I complete this book, I realize just how much that the safety profession has meant to me. For all the many people who had faith in me and allowed me to venture into new ways and styles of management...I am grateful! I hope that those that read this book may be inspired to challenge themselves to explore the many different concepts that I write about. As the title reads, proof of concept is indeed alive and well in my safety world. What about yours? Are you willing to take a chance to better your profession. I respectfully challenge you!

The mission of *Safety Program Management* is to educate the worker, employer, general public, and, most of all, you, the safety manager.

Appendix

Counseling Influences in Occupational Safety

David J. Nolting
Loyola University
1998

Abstract

The use of counselors in the occupational setting should be an effective attempt in controlling the startling numbers of workers that are injured and killed each year in the United States. The traditional safety person has vast knowledge of requirements and resources that aid in training and control of hazards in the workplace, but pure understanding of human factors is not an area of experience that most are afforded. The one common thread among all accidents that injure and kill is people. Understanding the human factors allows for interventions that address the needs of an ever-changing workforce. With downsizing and quality expectations, workers today are not viewed as they once were. Meeting deadlines and reducing cost are at the center of attention in most businesses today. The human side of industry gets lost in the shuffle, and needs go unmet. Such circumstances promote an atmosphere of discontent and worthlessness for the worker. People's interactions and interventions are necessary to meet the twenty-first-century workplace, and employing professional counselors to assess workplace situations allows for a better understanding of how and why accidents occur. This angle of intervention can be utilized in many different areas of the workplace, and this study will address several of these ideas.

Chapter 1

Counseling Influences in Occupational Safety

Can the use of counselors in the occupational safety setting be a useful tool in creating a safer environment for employees to work in? This interaction between counseling professionals and people in the workforce should not only be a reactive relationship but rather one that takes a proactive stand toward educating and training workers to perform their duties safely and efficiently. Who better than a professional counselor could understand the stresses and attitudes that affect a person's performance? Our society has finally recognized the need for mental health counselors in our private lives, but what about the need for assistance in an equally time-consuming part of life? We as an employed workforce spend as much time on average with our employer and coworkers than we do with our own families. Helping individuals and companies alike to recognize the human issues that influence our interactions can bridge the gap between personal life and employment responsibilities.

Statement of the Problem

This study will examine the need for counseling interaction and influences in the occupational workforce regarding safety issues. The following will expound on the several areas of safety that are critical aspects of performing work in a safe and productive manner.

Purpose of this Study

The purpose of this study is to answer the following questions: First, are human factors responsible for how employees perform their job tasks? Second, is understanding how a person's attitude affects the outcome of promoting a safe work environment and living up to such standards? Third, what role can a professional counselor play in effecting positive results in securing a safe workplace for all employees?

Hypotheses

For the purpose of this study, the following hypothesis will be tested: H Group and individual counseling can be a useful tool in aiding safety professionals to assess performance-related issues that affect why a person will react in a certain manner or how to train individuals to change pattern behaviors that create negative results.

Justification of the Study

Safety on any jobsite should be considered the most important issue to address in all phases of work to be performed. Workers are the most-valued asset of any company and should be recognized as a critical component in performing work in a productive, profitable, and safe manner. This philosophy should be the foundation of all businesses and addressed in the most effective way possible. Allowing professional counselors to assess and train workers how to perform their duties in an enjoyable, safe, and productive manner will create an atmosphere that should ultimately affect a company's profitability and reputation.

Counselors are involved in safety-related issues, such as "Return-to-Work" and "Employee Assistance Programs," but are rarely involved in designing a positive attitude-based for workers to perform in. Employee Assistance Programs usually engage a more symptomatic treatment plan rather than trying to improve performance by addressing other contributing factors that may directly affect a worker's abilities (Lewis, J., 1998, p. 264). The need for understanding how counseling workers to better understand themselves and their abilities can greatly aid in reducing hazards that are present when human factors are the motivating force for work related accidents.

Chapter 2

Review of Related Literature

Early Days of Safety

Safety on the job has been addressed throughout history, dating back as far as AD 23. During this time period, animal bladders were used as dust masks when working in quarries and other areas that exposed workers to high levels of dust. In AD 162, the first occupational disease was diagnosed as relating to work environments, and in 1775, cancer of the scrotum was diagnosed as relating to work conditions and was linked to men employed as chimney sweeps. Occupational medicine was first studied back in 1910 in the US and initiated the beginning of an era that recognized certain trades that exposed workers to known hazards. During the industrial revolution, machines and equipment were designed to perform work most productively without consideration for what hazards the operator might be exposed to. As time went on, many men were being killed in the workplace, with the Bureau of Labor Statistics in 1907 reporting that between 15,000 and 17,000 deaths were occurring each year. Much notice was given to these startling figures and caught the attention of the federal government, realizing that controls needed to be implemented to offset the high rate of deaths that were resulting from unsafe work conditions. The movement began in 1950 to study the problems associated with work hazards and thus led to the Occupational Safety and Health Act (OSHA) of 1970. OSHA was established in 1971 to set and explore standards for safety in the workplace. The intention of this act was to assist the worker in forcing the employer to furnish safer work environments and to defend any worker who is forced to work in unsafe conditions (Morgan, M., 1997, p. 236).

As the twentieth century is nearing its end, new and improved ideas need to be studied to address the ever-troubling problem of ensuring workers a safe place to facilitate their job tasks. Today's times affords the worker equipment and machinery that is on the "cutting edge" of technology and allows for a safer environment to apply their skills. But the one aspect that will always be a driving force in worker safety plays its role in the form of attitudes. As safety professionals and counselors become more aware of their own unique contributions to occupational safety, and learn how to integrate their skills and knowledge, a more educated workforce may evolve to meet the demanding twenty-first century for quality, profitable, and safely performed jobs.

Safety Engineering: A Changing Profession

Safety over the last thirty years has seen many changes take place. Addressing attitude issues has been talked about for many years. "Our safety attitude is the fundamental, determining reason for our safety behavior, much as some attitude is the reason for any other behavior we exhibit. In general, attitudes are the results of experiences we have had, and they are largely emotional learnings although habits and learnings from experience are also part of attitudes" (Hannaford, E., 1967, p. 217). Just as other reasons may be the driving force behind the way we act in other situations, understanding how and why human factors motivate our actions can be a catalyst to promote safe behavior. Attitude is the potential for action, and it depends on how we handle the situation that defines a safe act. In today's workforce, it is critical that communication play a key role in educating the everyday worker on positive approaches to job tasks. The days of sending workers out in the field or on the factory floor, ill prepared and in unsafe work conditions, are ways of the past. Sure, there are still those companies that stretch the limitations and rules that demand safe conditions, but the average employee has choices that can help facilitate action to control most hazardous exposures. Liability compensation for injured employees ranks as one of the top three factors that affect the financial stability of any company (Morgan, M., 1997, p. 237). Insurance companies, OSHA, DOT, EPA, and a host of similar agencies monitor the workplace to ensure compliance.

As the changing workplace reveals a streamlined approach to efficiency and quality, an evolution has also taken place in the safety profession to meet the needs of the twenty-first century. New programs have been developed to address safety-related issues concerning behavior change and total organizational approaches to offset negative human influences. These approaches address the need for total involvement within an organization to cooperate and implement a mindset that promotes safe behavior (Mathis & Spitzer, 1996, p. 6). Although these programs have proved to be useful tools in controlling breakdowns in safe behavior, they do not seem to fully reinforce the attitudes on a continuum. Another drawback appears to be in the area of execution, which either puts a strain on a company's safety budget or relies on safety professionals to train and evaluate a workforce in an area that they do not fully understand. To fully develop and implement a plan that effectively controls human factors that cause accidents depends on a dedication to the basic principles of performance-based safety. Such basics include assessment, management briefings, strategic planning, leadership development, and a long checklist that consumes much of an administrations time (Mathis & Spitzer, 1996, p. 24).

Many companies employ people in positions that take on numerous roles. Adding more responsibilities to an already full agenda may lead to certain areas suffering due to the inability to address all issues simultaneously. Understanding the reasons behind motivation and attitude are the fundamentals of inspiring people to change behaviors and to feel that the positive outcomes are worth the efforts put forth. With this understood, the premise of this study will address the usefulness and expertise that professional counselors bring to the safety industry. Counselors already play a role in some aspects in the occupational setting, such as rehabilitation services, but a broader approach can aid in the creation of a safe approach to not only workplace safety but in a manner that prevents a potential problem from becoming a statistic.

Recognizing Human Factors

Human factors account for our uniqueness and individuality. No two people are alike, and in turn what motivates one may not motivate another. Recognizing certain characteristics of employees can result in proper job assignment and the reduction of work-related accidents. Placing individuals in positions that are not suited for their abilities does not only mean that a person may lack skills in that particular area. Improper job placement because of a personality or attitude difference may limit the necessary functioning level that may be required to perform that job task in a safe manner. Leo DeBobes writes, "An individual of average or above-average intelligence is not a good candidate for a routine, monotonous job because boredom itself leads to carelessness and risk taking" (DeBobes, L., 1996). Aggressiveness, passivity, and type-A personalities can be as disruptive to an operation as unsafe environmental conditions. Unsafe or negative situations can destroy a safety program quicker than it was developed.

The role of the counselor in this setting tests the same structures as do the family therapist. Family counseling is concerned with not only what appears on the outside but also how the family functions as a whole. Family subsystems are a critical component of any healthy family, but knowing and living within certain boundaries are essential to positive growth (Corey, G., 1996, p. 394). As in the family setting, the workforce has its own subsystem and boundaries that rely on precise interaction to achieve competitive and profitable results. Understanding the rudiments of positive functioning is where a counselor separates themselves from the traditional safety professional. Incorporating human factors into a safety program when designing one can be very helpful in understanding the essential needs that a safety program has when operating within a predictive methodology. Following the leader is most commonly referred to as a child's game, but for most people, followers are more common than leaders. Establishing a relationship with a natural born leader that draws upon his/her qualities can be a tremendous aid in setting a positive tone for the rest of the employees. Not always will the natural leader be the boss but simply that negative person who keeps a safety program on edge. Empowering that person to become a positive role model is not an impossible task to accomplish. People have a need to be recognized, and turning around the pessimistic reveler gives them a sense of recognition which ultimately may lead to a productive and caring worker. To many, perception is reality, but understanding why certain behaviors exist can be a crucial role of counselors in the occupational environment.

Counselors are trained to observe a person as multidimensional, with many dynamics that account for personality and behavior traits. Modern approaches in the mental-health field have shown that people can be in control of their lives and that choices can be made to overcome obstacles to meet their goals. Existential therapy deals with the "here and now" issues and helps empower people to set goals and to gain freedom over their lives (Corey, G., 1996, p. 172). When dealing with human nature, one should expect people to act in a "normal" way. When a worker gets defensive over a conversation with his/her supervisor regarding disciplinary actions, we tend to say it is natural to be angry. But if the angry attitude overcomes the reason for the scolding, then it is more than likely that the negative behavior may continue. Conversely, approaching an employee in a more constructive way may lead to solutions that help control potential problems in the workplace. The worker then tends to exhibit a more positive attitude. Helping workers to overcome frustrations in the job place allows for a better communication between employees and management. Sometimes, it's how something is said that makes more of an impact than what was said (Hannaford, E., 1967).

Communication needs to be clear and positive when trying to establish a mindset that promotes safe work habits. Counseling professionals understand human needs and are capable of addressing the special issues in such a way that promotes motivation to perform in a positive manner. Motivation may be all that a worker lacks, not ability. Motivation is encouraging a person to want to do something a certain way, not just because they have to.

Stress-Related Issues in the Workplace

In order to create a total safety mindset in the workplace, there needs to be a desire to do job tasks correctly and safely to avoid accidents. Recognizing the different levels of stress that accompanies the workplace is key in incorporating strategies to control hazards that exist. The average daily operation produces a minimum amount of stress, and the repetitive ongoing safety program usually is all that is needed to control and maintain safe attitudes by the workers. Short-term emotional upsets in the workplace, such as personnel disputes, can undermine a safe attitude unless the safety attitude has a strong base to outlast trying times. When the unexpected occurs and panic sets in, we as humans rely on our instincts to defend against outside influences. Without a strong safety attitude, one that becomes instinctive, our sense of safety ceases to operate, thus allowing for hazards to affect the outcome of the event. In a "nutshell," repetitive safety awareness over time becomes instinctive and reactive in positive ways to negative stimuli.

Addressing stress-related concerns in the workplace is not as easy as creating a packaged intervention program to tackle all issues. Instead, a tailored program that addresses the unique situation in a given organization can be more useful when targeting specific issues

(Baker, E. & at al., 1996). This form of interaction is not easily dealt with by nonmental health professionals since training in this area is quite intensive and experiential. The traditional safety professional may not understand what makes one position more stressful than another. With this in mind, counselors would benefit any organization intent on designing a proactive, solution-oriented safety program. Recognizing stress-related issues sometimes mean more than observing the position but rather analyzing the individual that performs the job. Counselors are well-aware of special needs and confidentiality issues that allow for more personal interaction than that between an employee and supervisor. Fear of reprisal my limit communication regarding unsafe conditions when talking to supervisors. Such relationships as the counselor/worker may pave the way for dealing with root causes of stress-related problems in the workplace. A study (Pendleton & Stotland, 1996) revealed that worker perception plays a large part of how stress affects the individual. Perceptions regarding job difficulty, challenges, stress in their personal lives, and life changes are all related to how a worker may deal with job-related stress. Counseling in the occupational setting can be just as effective as in the mental health setting when facilitating theory-approached methodology.

Treating stress in the workplace has been met with positive responses from employers in many large business settings. Such treatment is usually geared toward dealing with the individual worker rather than redesigning an entire organization. For this reason, being cost-effective makes it a viable avenue in targeting individuals with particular issues that may only affect a few (Murphy & Sorenson, 1988). Counselors using behavioral modification techniques to facilitate a treatment plan should be acknowledged by the safety industry as a professional approach to a never-ending symptom of strain-related illnesses do to stress on the job. Behavioral techniques allow the worker to better handle stress and learn relaxation strategies that relieve tension in all areas of their lives.

In a research paper published by Lawrence Murphy, David Dubois, and Joseph Hurrell (1986): To the extent that stress contributes to accident occurrences, strategies designed to prevent or reduce stress may have potential for decreasing accident risk and find value as adjuncts to safety-training programs. In this regard, a number of recent studies have evaluated prescriptive, relaxation-based methods for helping workers recognize and manage stress. Techniques include biofeedback, muscle relaxation, meditation, and cognition-focused methods, many of which were borrowed from clinical practice where they have been used successfully to treat psychosomatic and psycho-physiological dysfunctions. As applied in work settings, these techniques have a distinct, preventive flavor with an emphasis on imparting skills to symptom-free workers. Accordingly, a stress management training (SMT) is more appropriately viewed as a health-promotion activity rather than as a treatment strategy for troubled workers (pp. 12–13).

Employees may be more productive when they understand why and how they react to one another or to certain situations. This could also impact the use of sick time, thus lowering medical cost for providers that treat illnesses related to occupational stress and strain.

Understanding Environmental and Special Case Influences

Understanding environmental factors allows safety management to better comprehend the issues that workers face due to uncommon situations. Such situations as night-shift work can affect one's ability to perform to their potential. Our bodies are on a time clock that aids in our sleep patterns. Normally, most people sleep during night hours and take care of their business in daylight. But when a person reverses the roles, something takes place in our bodies that throws off our biorhythms. In an article depicting health services for shift and night workers (Koller, 1996), it is suggested that occupational health services which include counseling be offered to the employee before the beginning of shift-work activities. This article even explored the Australian night-shift work-law regulation of 1981, revised in 1993, where night workers are entitled to special health assessments, more leisure time, and even early retirement possibilities depending on how long exposed. Although this previous statement is employee-friendly, one may defend the position that over time, our bodies adapt to changes and symptoms disappear.

Another occupational concern to be explored is the "critical incident" worker. Such workers fall under different categories, with one common thread, disasters. When these people go to work, the level of energy is high, and workers usually don't settle down until life and property are secure. In the Oklahoma bombing, most of those workers remained on the job for days at a time, and it was not uncommon for this type of operation to last several days and even weeks. When ice storms hit the Louisiana, Mississippi, and Tennessee areas a few years ago, the power company and its contractors stayed on the job working sixteen-hour days until power was restored to all the communities. Only after a couple of long workdays and short nights workers become irritable, slower to react, and disoriented at times. It is before the worker gets to that point that assistance be offered to address the anxieties and emotions that the workers experience due to these critical incident responses. Add the long workdays with observing devastation and death, and you have a combination that will work on the minds of most people.

Counselors are often brought into these situations for aiding the victims of the disaster but not always are the disaster workers recognized as potential victims themselves. The American Red Cross has mental-health professionals that respond to disaster areas, with the main focus on apparent victims who have been traumatized by the loss of life and property. If occupational counselors are teamed with the rescue and recovery personnel to provide services, such as debriefings and relaxation techniques, a close observation can be conducted to help recognize problems brewing before they become accidents. Each occupation has its unique operational procedures, and understanding what they are will aid the counselor to fully be aware of the limitations of the job task to ensure that the worker operates within his/her boundaries.

Last, but not the least, dealing with post-traumatic stress syndrome (PTSS) should be on the agenda of all response operations that work under critical conditions. Counselors who are aware of specific operations may be helpful in training workers on what to expect and how to deal with traumatic events while on the job or in their personal lives. Using therapeutic techniques, such as cognitive approaches, can assist in the nurturing of a safe sense of well-being and awareness that may cushion exposure to such events (Dobson & Craig, 1996, pp. 249–250).

Addressing special needs in the workplace encompasses a variety of situations, which could include mediation services. Mediation involves workplace disputes, employee assistance programs, and problem areas that require an unbiased opinion that would weigh both sides to seek solutions to disruptive incidents (Greenstone & Leviton, 1996). Counselors who have such training would play a productive role in empowering an organization to maintain a positive environment for all to work in. Crisis situations are another area that may be addressed by counselors that may involve serious injuries or deaths to business employees. Just as in the school systems of many cities, counselors could be brought in to counsel workers that either experienced tragic events or were friends with those that were affected.

Substance Abuse in the Workplace

Accidents that are occurring in the workplace happen four times more frequently when drugs and alcohol are involved. Several other areas, such as high absenteeism, high insurance cost, poor job performance, and low-quality production, are all results of substance abuse. These issues are only a few of the problems that companies face when employees try to buck the system and work while under the influence. Since the introduction of drug-testing programs, the rate of related incidents has gone down, but valued employees are being affected every day. Employee assistance programs (EAP) affords the worker a resource to help them get sober, but most programs are outside agencies that may treat the worker as just another patient. In-house programs staffed with a counselor who has experience in these areas can be greatly beneficial to the safety and production operation of a company that is interested in establishing and maintaining a safety, conscious atmosphere for all its employees. With in-house staff, employees have access to professional help that should be able to lend itself to a much broader approach to the entire situation. With team approach methods, the employee has an opportunity to address many issues at one time (Bensinger, P., 1985).

Counseling Workers Needs

By staffing an organization with a professional counselor needs not otherwise recognized by the lay person may be addressed. In an article written (Haas, 1977) about learning real feelings, the issue of fears and anxieties were studied. The essay researched true feelings that high steel-iron workers had about their job and how they confronted them. This study pointed out that most workers, though afraid, worked at great heights without trying to express fear due to a sense of macho mentality. These workers went about their daily routine acting as if the high workplace was not a problem but rather dealing with an anxiety that created a stress that they dare not talk about. This fear of talking out seemed to make them feel that their coworkers would ridicule them or refuse to work by their side. If workers in these situations were afforded the opportunity to confront their problems within the context of a group setting, counselors could be very instrumental in facilitating such avenues of anxiety relief.

Many other areas of assistance could be helpful to employees, but the one most important issue raised is the notion that when these proactive programs are made available to the workforce, a sense of caring is portrayed by the organization. This alone could be a strong influence on how workers perform their job tasks.

Workplace Violence

Workplace violence rears its ugly head in many different forms, but the one that this researcher is interested in is directly related to the job setting. Preventing violence on the job requires a constant awareness of situations before they develop and get out of hand. According to previous research, accidents are still the number-one cause for deaths in the workplace, but 12 percent of those deaths are reported to be related to criminal activity (Thomas, J. 1992).

Understanding stress issues and how to defuse potential problems can play a major role in reducing these types of workplace injuries or deaths. When employees are demoted, laid off, or fired from a job, special attention needs to be given to assess the situation and the individual. In many cases, an employee's self-esteem and job are tied to one another, and when this string is broken, the employee may feel a sense of worthlessness. As this occurs, if the employee does not have a strong support system in their personal life, the employee may try to blame others for his/her failures, thus taking it out on coworkers and supervisors. It is not so uncommon anymore for one to turn the television on and see that a disgruntled ex-employee went into his former workplace and killed someone. A trained eye may have noticed the telltale signs of violence brewing ("Preventing Violence in the Workplace," 1994).

Professional counselors could be contracted to deal with issues relating to these types of situations and could make experienced evaluations regarding possible interventions to potential problems. Sometimes, supervisors become emotionally involved and fail to see the clear picture, thus looking right past a violent situation.

Counseling Accident Prevention

Training individuals and groups to perform their jobs in a safe manner implies a long-term approach that involves many different areas of concentration. One area that has proved to be useful is in the form of goal setting and feedback. When implementing a safety program, involving the entire organization is wise to encourage and motivate all employees to work safely. If goals that are difficult but attainable are set through interaction of the labor force, then half of the battle has been won. A follow-up on attaining those certain goals need to be in the form of feedback. Such feedback allows the workers to see where they stand and requires them to take responsibility for their own actions.

Another area approach that may be helpful involves the techniques of coaching strategies. When an athletic coach targets a certain game plan to attack an oncoming opponent, all aspects of the game are addressed. Not only weaknesses are addressed but strong points as well. When devising a viable approach to defeating the opposing team, a good coach must first look within and pick out the possibilities that exist when developing a plan of action. Certainly, a good coach would not suggest a game plan that its players could not possibly execute. Being realistic in the action plan is a key part of the process (Geller, E., 1996, p. 123).

In putting this idea to use in the occupational setting, planning goals could be attained if all players, workers, and supervisors would be realistic in selecting goals to strive for. Understanding human factors and communicating weaknesses and strong points to all involved aids in clarifying what and how a program will operate. By communicating feedback to employees as to how they are doing, a sense of curiosity develops and competitiveness among different sections of an organization as well. Awarding incentives encourages workers to be aware of appreciation that a business might have for safely performed work and to create a sense of purpose for working safely.

One drawback to coaching strategies in the safety setting is that unlike sports, people usually view this sort of interaction as a personal confrontation. This is where the need for professional counselors could be beneficial, addressing individuals in nonthreatening ways to safety-sensitive issues. Proactive training in these areas prepares workers for future interaction should it be necessary that they be singled out for correction on safety performance in the workplace.

Operating within these perimeters creates a team approach to safe work practices that once was concerned with individual actions.

This style of approach is indeed similar to that of the cognitive theory where choices are made and behavior changes are presented to attain goals that are set. Counselors help empower people to gain control of their lives and in turn can be applied to the worker or group that is intent on achieving set goals. This is just another area among many that could benefit with the assistance of professional counselors who are trained to understand people.

A professional working relationship between a safety manager and counselor has many possibilities that could elevate the proactive approach to safety to another level. Such relationships could play a vital role in attending to the safety needs of men and women that perform job tasks in today's workplace. When combining both fields of knowledge, an extensive understanding of the intricate needs that must be met to develop and maintain a proactive and successful safety program are realized. Safety professionals are faced with many obstacles each day when trying to conduct safety management in all forms of business. With this understood, counselors would be helpful in handling select issues that would relieve the safety professional to attend to the everyday responsibilities of the operation for which they are in charge. Counselors handling human-based issues would integrate the how and why into a safety program. It is not enough to just mandate safety policies, but communicating the reasons behind the rules are an essential part of the success of accomplishing compliance among the workforce.

Developing Change: Team Attitude

Attitudes are the basic motivation to the success of any safety program, and without a positive one, little can be accomplished. If a counselor was to embrace the existential approach toward teaching employees to perform safe work, the premise would be to address the here and now. Changes are inevitable, and it is how we handle them that makes all the difference in the world. Developing a program for an organization to follow in order to provide a safe work environment needs the cooperation of all. Every person from the top to bottom should be involved so that the entire organization is working toward the same goals to achieve a level of compliance that is welcomed by the workforce and not due to fear of reprisal. Team attitudes work great in athletic events and do so because there is group participation. All involved are working toward executing the desired play or plan of action. Without team attitude, it is quite easy for an organization to lose focus of the goals that they are working toward. Counselors are trained in understanding how to empower people to find the solutions to life's problems, and applying the same principles to the work setting could be a viable avenue in assisting business to accomplish safety performance that promotes quality, profitable, and safely performed work. Attitudes can make or break a company, and addressing related issues in positive ways can only encourage safe performance.

Summary

In summary, communicating to workers that there are usually two ways that work can be performed, the possible way and the probable way, gives them an idea of choices that can be made when performing their job task. Most workers in the workplace have the ability to perform their job task by the book, but unfortunately, most of us skip steps, thus walking on that proverbial fence between safety and disaster. When a person goes to get their driver's license for the first time, they do all the necessary things needed to pass the driving test, but weeks later, that same person becomes comfortable with what's going on and steps are deleted from their driving habits. Changing lanes or pulling out from side streets seem less threatening than before. It is during these times that most accidents occur when you feel invincible or lose respect for the dangers involved when driving a vehicle.

This same attitude applies to the occupational setting and could be communicated as a training tool. Bridging the gap between the possible and the probable would help create a more solid intervention strategy for controlling hazards and promoting safety awareness. The aid of professional counselors in the occupational setting could benefit the safety industry in addressing employee attitudes and human factors that influence the work environment. The premise of this idea is based upon the fact that most safety professionals have a wealth of knowledge when it comes to safety in the workplace but little understanding about human factors that can either make or break a safety program. By employing counselors to intervene at only critical times merely addresses part of the problem that dangers in the workplace pose. If counselors are given the opportunity to be part of an action plan that starts at the proactive end, and follows a program across the spectrum throughout its existence, a more cohesive relationship may evolve between the worker and management.

It was reported recently in *USA Today* that the US House of Representatives Committee on Small Business estimates that approximately seventeen workers die and that 18,600 are injured every day in the workplace. It would appear that these large numbers are indicators that traditional approaches are not effective enough to control hazards that create these startling statistics. By approaching safety issues in a way that addresses the root causes for most accidents, one cannot but understand that people control the workplace, not machines. Who better than professional counselors have the edge to these intervention techniques?

References

Baker, E., L. Goldenhar, C. Heaney, and B. Isreal. 1996. "Occupational Stress, Safety, and Health: Conceptual Framework and Principles for Effective Prevention Interventions." *Journal of Occupational Health Psychology*, 1(3), 261–286.

Bensinger, P. 1985. "Drugs in the Workplace: A Commentary." *Behavioral Sciences & the Law*, 3(4), 441–453.

Corey, G., 1996. *Theory and Practice of Counseling and Psychotherapy*. Pacific Grove, California: Brooks/Cole Publishing Company.

Craig, K. and K. Dobson, eds. 1996. *Advances in Cognitive-Behavioral Therapy*. Thousand Oaks, California: Sage Publications, Inc.

DeBobes, L. 1986. "The Work Environment: The Psychological Factors in Accident Prevention." *Personnel Journal*, January 1986.

DeReamer, R. 1958. *Modern Safety Practices*. New York, New York: John Wiley & Sons, Inc.

Dubois, D., J. Hurrell, and L. Murphy. 1986. "Accident Reduction through Stress Management." *Journal of Business and Psychology*, 1(1), 5–18.

Greenstone, J. and S. Leviton. 1997. *Elements of Mediation*. Pacific Grove, California: Brooks/Cole Publishing Company.

Geller, E. S. 1996. *The Psychology of Safety*. Radnor, Pennsylvania: Chilton Book Company.

Haas, J. 1977. "Learning Real Feelings." *Journal of Sociology of Work and Occupations*, 4(2), 147–169.

Hannaford, E. 1967. *Supervisor's Guide to Human Relations*. Chicago, Illinois: National Safety Council.

Koller, M. 1996. "Occupational Health Services for Shift and Night Workers." *Journal of Applied Ergonomics*, 27(1), 31–37.

Mathis, T. and D. Spitzer. 1996. *Developing a Safety Culture: Successfully Involving the Entire Organization*. Neenah, Wisconsin: J.J. Keller & Associates, Inc.

Morgan, M. 1997. *Environmental Health*. Englewood, Colorado: Morton Publishing Company.

Murphy, L. and S. Sorenson. 1988. "Employee Behaviors Before and After Stress Management." *Journal of Organizational Behavior*, 9, 173–182.

Lewis, J., M. Lewis, J. Daniels, and M. D'Andrea. 1998. *Community Counseling: Empowerment Strategies for a Diverse Society*. Pacific Grove, California: Brooks/Cole Publishing Company.

Pendleton, M. and E. Stotland. 1989. "Workload, Stress, and Strain among Police Officers." *Journal of Behavioral Medicine*, spring 1989.

"Preventing Violence in the Workplace," 1994. USA: Bureau of Business Practice.

Thomas, J. 1992. "Occupational Violent Crime: Research on an Emerging Issue." *Journal of Safety Research*, 23, 55–62.